PARIS-ORLY AIRPORT
100 YEARS

FRÉDÉRIC BENIADA

PARIS-ORLY AIRPORT
100 YEARS

FRÉDÉRIC BENIADA

ABRAMS | NEW YORK

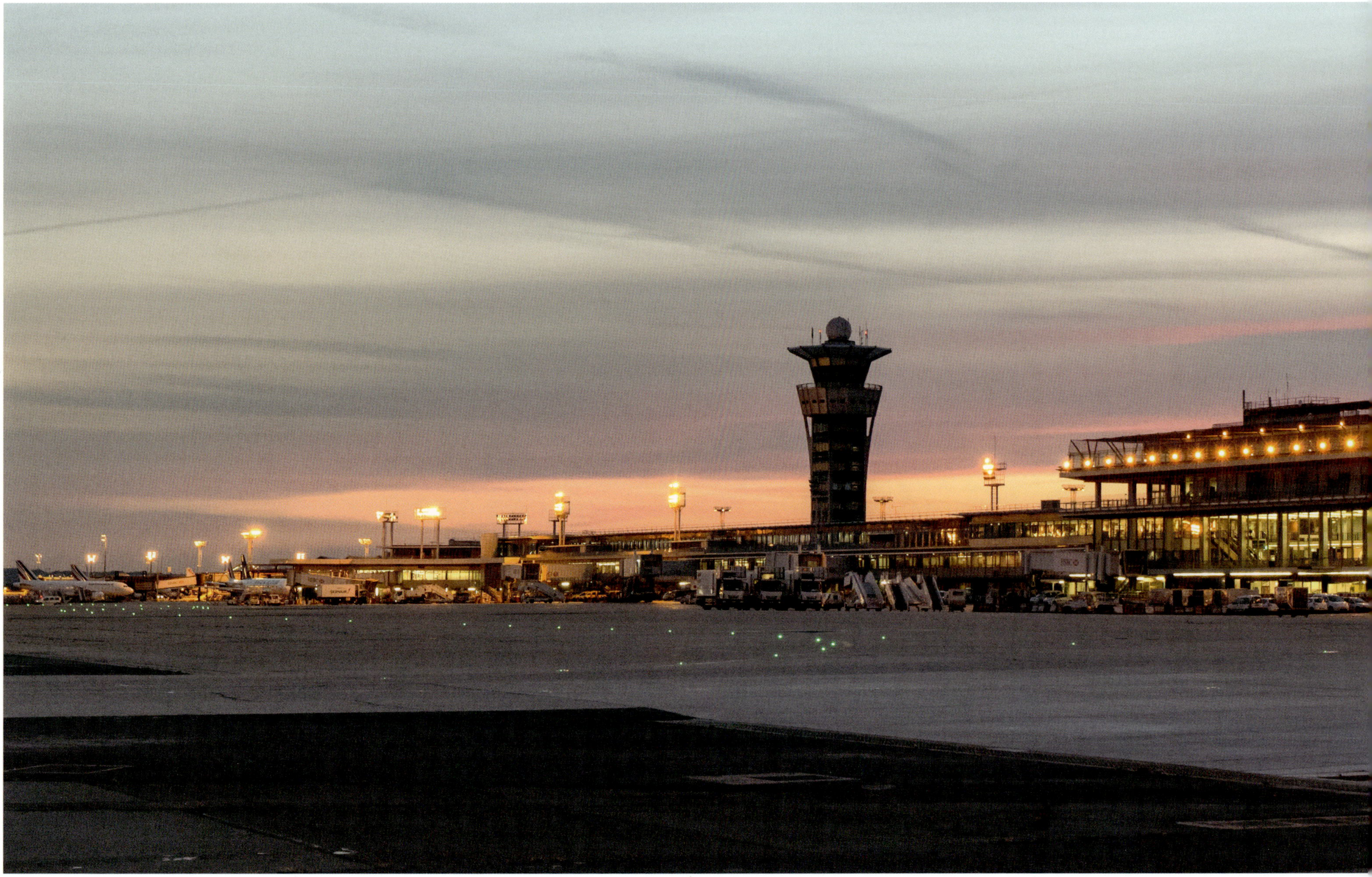

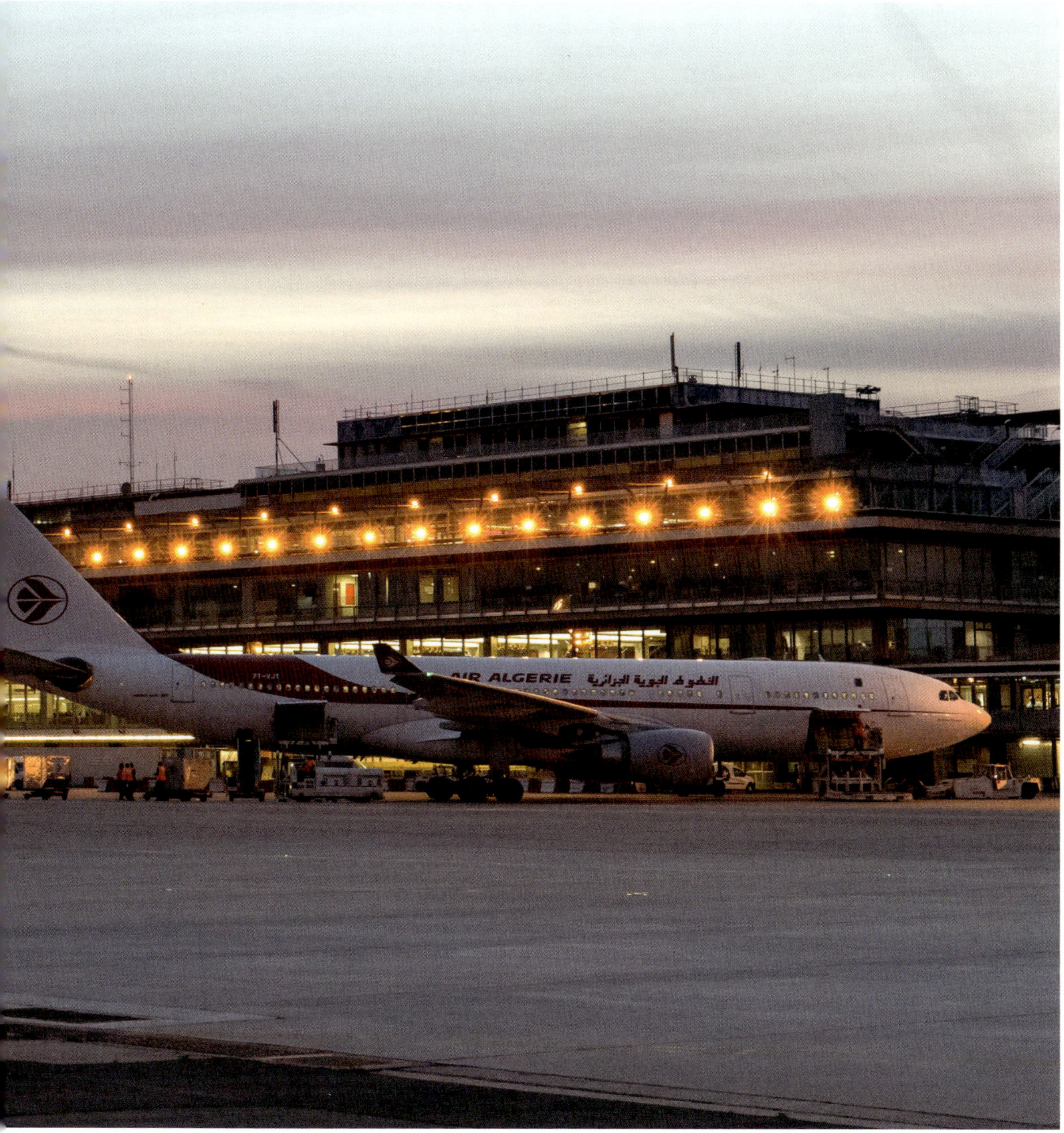
AIR ALGERIE الخطوط الجوية الجزائرية

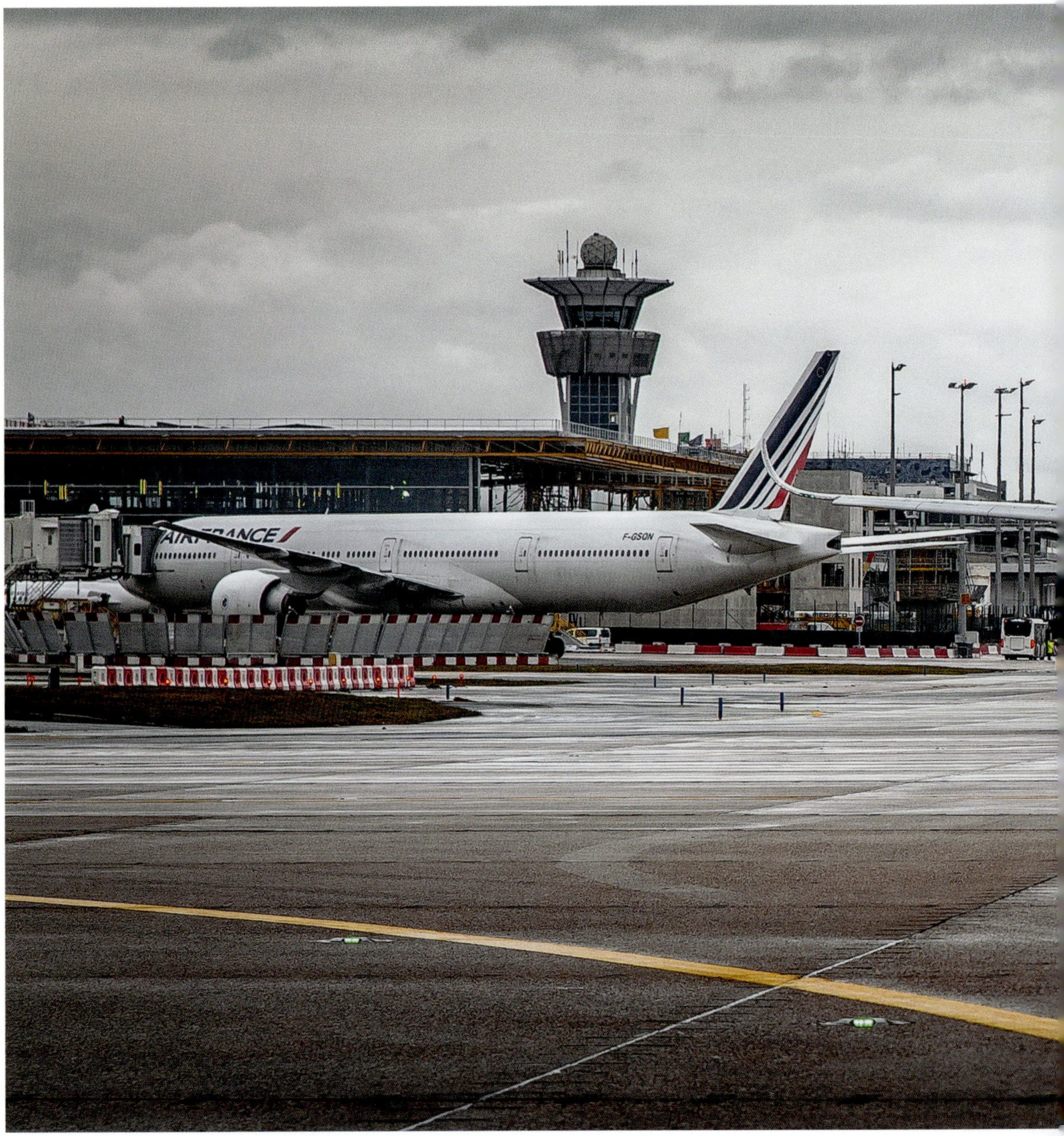
AIR FRANCE
F-GSQN

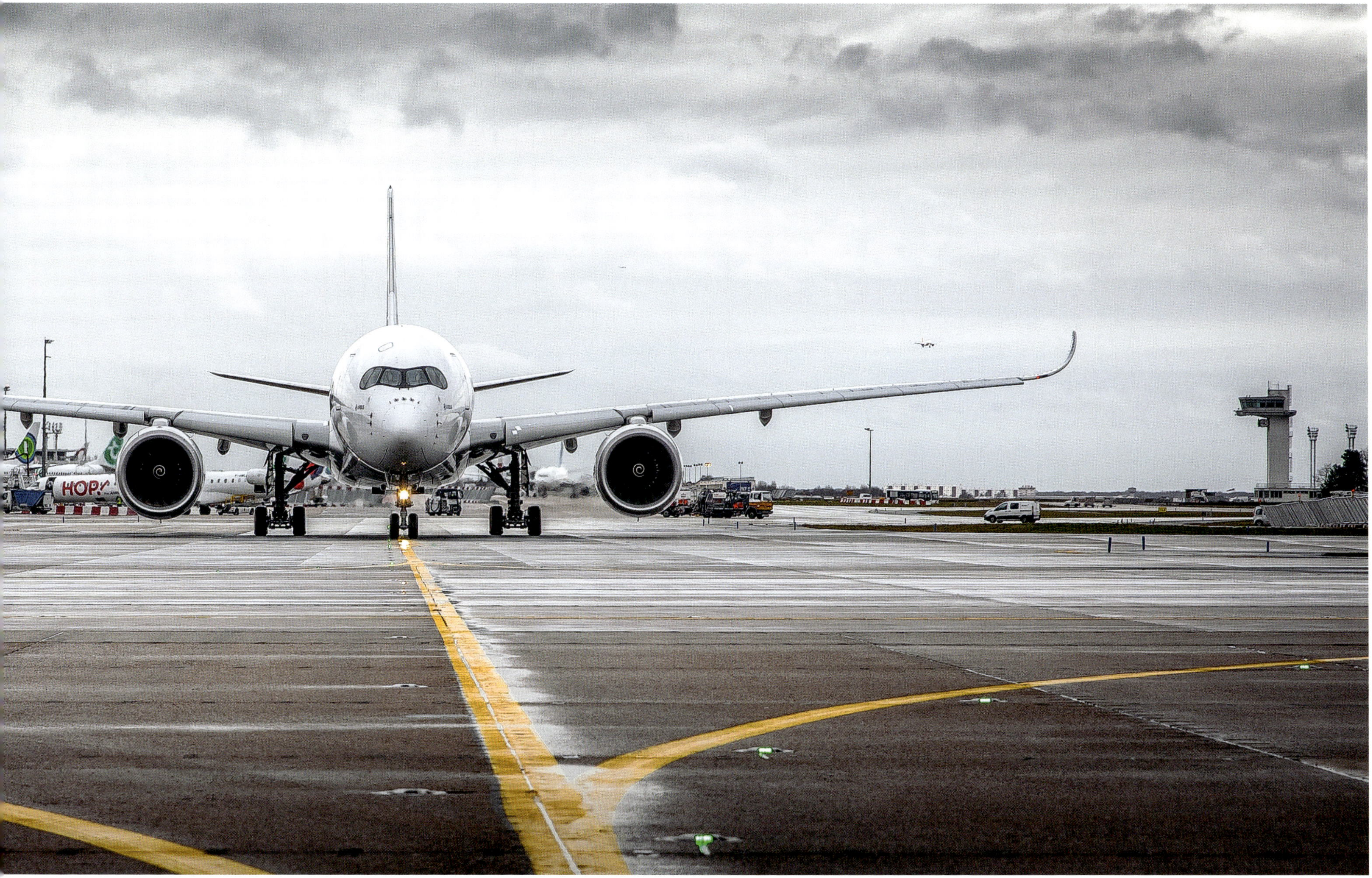
HOP!

FOR 100 YEARS, PARIS-ORLY HAS LED THE WAY

Paris-Orly Airport was officially born on 1 January 1918. That was the moment that War minister Georges Clemenceau requisitioned 11 hectares of land on the Plateau de Longboyau and ordered the construction of a single hangar. Little did he imagine the extraordinary epic that lay ahead – a full century of technical and cultural innovations, wrought by men and women who were passionate about flying, travel and freedom.

In this book by Frédéric Beniada you will discover the large and small historical details of those unsung exploits that have forged the soul of Paris-Orly.

In 1961, General de Gaulle opened Orly South. The new terminal designed by Henri Vicariot revolutionized airport architecture. Innovation, culture, the hopes of those times and the modernity are everywhere to be seen: cinema screen, luxury shops, restaurants ... Daring and the spirit of innovation blow powerfully through every dimension of the project. The public took to it, and the terminal became the most visited attraction in France, ahead of the Eiffel Tower. Then ten months later, after forty months of work, Orly West added the final piece to the undertaking.

Today with that same spirit of innovation we are writing a new page in the history of Paris-Orly. From runways to terminals, a profound metamorphosis is taking place, creating a new experience for tomorrow, for the benefit of passengers and airlines alike. New hotels, a business complex accessed by a futuristic walkway, a new pier for international flights ... these projects are already realities that bring to life the previously theoretical concept of the airport conceived as a town.

But the best is yet to come. In 2019, an 80,000m^2 building will connect the South Terminal to the West Terminal. Next will come a building to receive the Paris Metro and the TGV in the heart of the site. This new infrastructure will change the face of Paris-Orly in profound ways.

In parallel, there's a digital revolution taking place. Every day, new technologies are changing the way the airport's public spaces work. Smart Airport, Connected Airport, face recognition ... Groupe ADP's teams are making Paris-Orly one huge connected entity that's more rational, more fluid, more energy-saving and more respectful of its environment. There's an accelerating connection with the cultural and economic world too, as musicians, artists, designers and start-up sponsors all lend their presence to the airport and invest the terminals with the spirit of the town.

With Paris-Charles de Gaulle and Le Bourget, Paris-Orly represents one part of a balanced and growing regional airport system. This complementary group represents a considerable advantage for our country.

Paradoxically, as we celebrate the 100th anniversary of Orly, it seems to me that the airport era is only just beginning. In ancient times there were the ports, then came the railway stations of the 19th century, then the freeways of the 20th century – and now the present century promises to be the century of the airports.

I wager that those who celebrate the 200th anniversary of Orly will be as fascinated as I am by the strength of the creative imagination that built it. They will look back on the history of Orly and understand the profound meaning of a quote from Virgil that I especially like: *Felix qui potuit rerum cognoscere causas*. Fortunate are those who understand the causes of things.

Enjoy the book.

Augustin de Romanet
President and director general of Groupe ADP

Orly
AÉROPORT DE PARIS

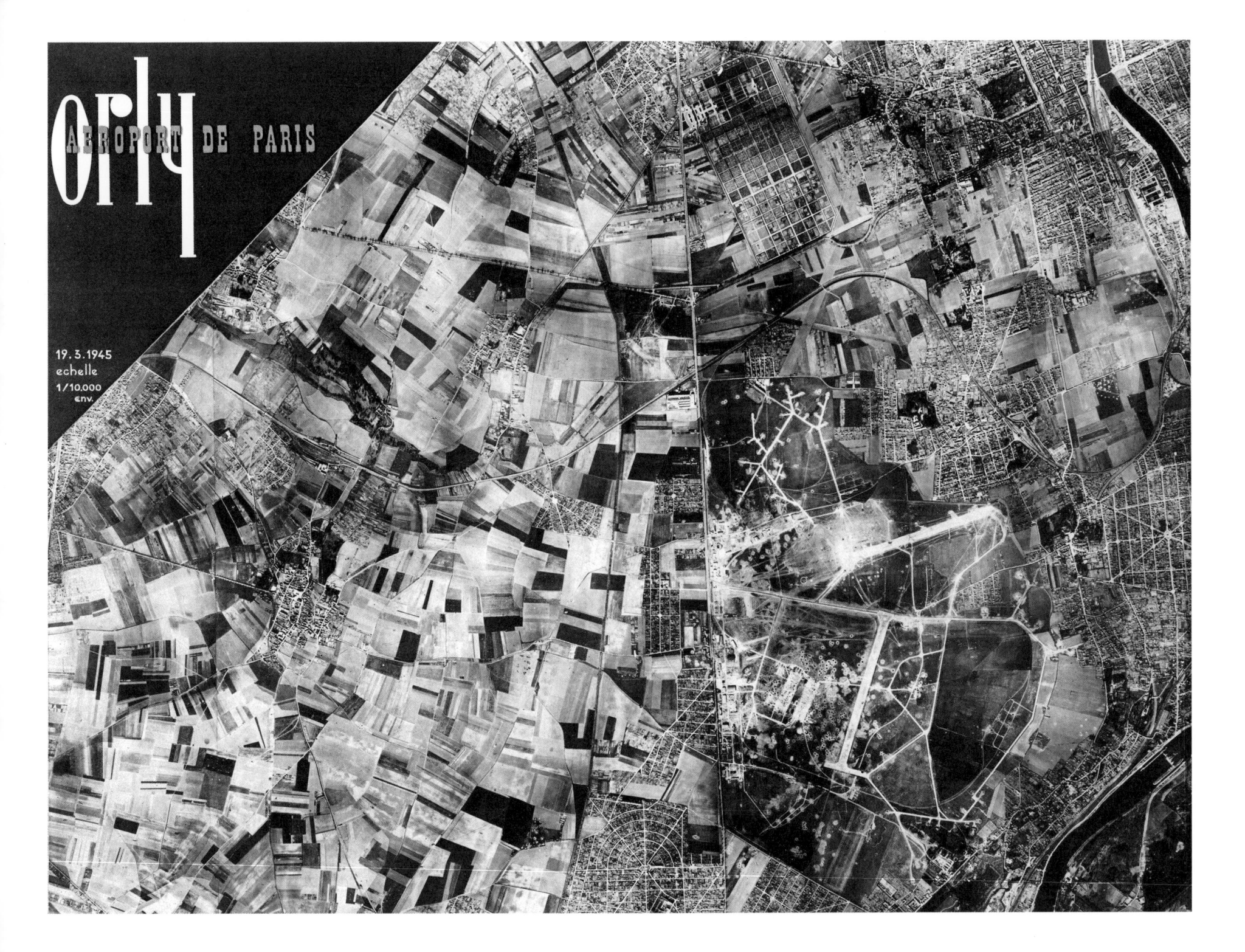

19.3.1945
echelle
1/10.000
env.

CONTENTS

12—BIRTH OF AN AIRPORT
1918-1945

32—COMMERCIAL AVIATION TAKES OFF
1945-1961

74—MODERNIZATION AND EXPANSION
1961-2000

104—THE AIRPORT IN THE CITY
PARIS-ORLY TODAY

152—AN AIRPORT LOOKING TO THE FUTURE
A FRESH START

Aerial view of Orly in 1945.

BIRTH OF AN AIRPORT

1918-1945

ORLY AIRPORT OPENED OFFICIALLY IN 1918.

But it was back in 1910 that the first flying machines took off from what started as a field surrounded by farms and several isolated houses. A year earlier, some members of parliament attracted by the exploits of the first aviators had joined to form the Société d'Encouragement à l'Aviation (association to promote flying, the SEA). Members then set about finding a large area of land close to Paris to accommodate the exploits of these flying madmen and their wild ambitions. The members were Alfred de Pischof, Léon Delagrange, Ferdinand Ferber, Clément Ader and Louis Paulhan. And so on 23 May 1909, in the commune of Viry Châtillon close to the Seine, Transport Minister Léon Barthou inaugurated Port Aviation, the world's first formally established aerodrome. To mark the occasion, the archbishop of Paris baptized two Voisin planes with the names *Île-de-France* and *Alsace-Lorraine*.

The 100-hectare site grew to be a huge flying field surrounded by numerous shops, restaurants, stands for competition spectators, a press room for reporters and even a telephone booth. In reality, this was more than a single flying field, with several spread around the communes of Villejuif to the north, Savigny to the south, Massy to the west and Villeneuve le Roi to the east, as far as the plateau of Longboyau. Port Aviation quickly became the venue for the first flying events, with the greatest of the pioneers taking part. Their exploits and racing attracted an ever-growing crowd of curious spectators. In the autumn of 1909, a fortnight of flying was organized in the style of the great Rheims flying week, with many prizes to be won. Constructors came to Port Aviation to test their prototypes. At the back of the hangars, they developed the first cockpit instruments, following the example of Adolphe Doutre and his automatic stabilizer, and the flying test-bed concept of Jean Legrand.

In 1910, the engineer Raymond Saulnier set up shop at Port Aviation. There he met Léon Morane, and together they founded the famous firm Morane-Saulnier, forerunner of Socata, today Daher-Socata. It was at Port Aviation that Louis Blériot prepared for his crossing of the Channel, and Léon Delagrange broke several distance and endurance records.

In the winter of 1910, the flying field was flooded by the rising waters of the Seine. Port Aviation was under water for several months, and this marked the beginning of its decline.

The flyers went looking for drier locations, such as the Champagne farm at Savigny sur Orge, the Contin farm at Paray Vieille Poste, and the farm at Filou on the Orly plateau. Over time activity at Port Aviation diminished, public interest weakened, and just before the War it was sold for development to an entrepreneur from Juvisy. The Orly flying field meanwhile grew in importance and several flying schools were established there. It was at Orly that Adolphe Pégoud first flew upside-down in his Blériot.

The First World War called a temporary halt to the dreams and exploits of these pioneers, who now had other matters on their minds. Pilots were assigned to their original military units unless they held a military pilot's license, and mechanics were attached to motorized army units. But with the First World War came a new concept – aerial combat – and such was the need for pilots, the government decided to revise its plans and introduced a new military pilot's qualification. To be selected and declared fit for aerial combat, you had to complete a flight of at least one hour at an altitude of 1000 meters, complete a gliding landing with the motor stopped, complete three test flights of more than 200 kilometers, and pass a theory exam. This new rule was a breath of fresh air. Training was three months maximum, on the Caudron G3. Those who failed the course were returned to their respective units. The French school soon attracted trainees from Belgian, Portugese and then American forces. Without the advent of aerial combat, Orly might never have seen the light of day.

Orly was easy to locate and accessible so at the beginning of the First World War the field served as an emergency landing ground for allied planes. The farmers of the plateau often saw them landing. In 1918, when the Americans had only recently joined the conflict, the Orly airfield became an American base. One hundred and sixty soldiers took charge of the necessary land and built a military camp. This was the point at which the real expansion of Orly commenced. Buildings and hangars were constructed for the training planes.

At the end of the war, the Americans returned the land and Orly became a civil aerodrome. In 1921, the air traffic service built a command centre to accommodate the management of the airport and its administrative services. The status of Orly was defined in the monthly publication Bulletin de la Navigation Aerienne (air traffic bulletin) under the title "The training of civil aviation pilots": "Reserve pilots may be trained at Orly, Angers, Orléans, Clermont-Ferrand or Bordeaux on planes of the Caudron G3 type."

It was at this time that the Service des Entrepôts Généraux de l'Aviation (SEGA) was established at Orly, followed by the equivalent service for the navy. These bodies were responsible for stocking aerial warfare supplies, and surplus destined for sale to civil customers, both businesses and individuals. The market in this surplus stock attracted industrial customers.

The first passenger aircraft now made their appearance on the site, taking advantage of the aerodrome's good road and rail connections. It was in this period that a group of manufacturers formed the Compagnie Aérienne Française (CAF). They operated flights on request, flying in a Farman Goliath F60 to Le Bourget, Buc, Villacoublay and Toussus le Noble. At the end of the 1920s, two huge hangars with space for two zeppelins were built at the top of Paray Vieille Poste. These airships, including the *Dixmude*, had been given to France by Germany as reparations after the War. The hangars were 300m long, 100m wide and 58m high, built using a new method of concrete construction developed by the engineer Eugène Freyssinet. The immense roof was constructed of castings that weighed several tons. The two buildings were completed in 1928. For the pilots, they represented a terrific landmark for navigation and, according to rumor, the more foolhardy among them would fly right through their immense open vaults.

Sadly, the two zeppelins were destroyed in accidents and the Aéroclub de France then took over the two hangars for testing their own balloons. At the request of the State, Charles Nungesser, an air ace with 43 air combat victories to his credit, set up a flying school to train one part of the quota. The best pilots would come from his school. Nungesser also offered air transport on request, via Nungesser Aviation whose slogan was: *Par n'importe quel temps! À n'importe quelle heure!* (In any weather! At any time!) The company established the Paris-Deauville route. But faced with competition from CAF, the Nungesser operation went bankrupt several years later.

It was still early days for aviation, yet barely 30 years on we were already talking of conservation. In 1923, the first fuel consumption trial was organized between Orly and Lyon. The Zénith cup was awarded to the pilot who completed the distance using the least quantity of fuel, at a speed of no less than 70kph. Under the aegis of the Aéroclub de France and the Fédération Aéronautique Internationale (FAI), an increasing number of competitions, challenges and fuel consumption trials were staged. The aim was to help develop passenger aviation. Orly was the birthplace of the Michelin Cup, the Dunlop Cup, the Paris-Saigon Challenge and the first round-France race for passenger aircraft.

Large loans were available to individuals to buy light French planes and, with the introduction of paid holidays in 1936, the government increased funding for the setting up of flying clubs open to everybody.

Clubs appeared in every quarter of the capital, attracting large numbers of young Parisians who now had considerably more money to spend. The Roland-Garros flying club was one of the largest among them, with nearly 200 members and 40 machines, the owners including Baron Amaury de la Grange, Colonel Wateau and General Denain. Exclusive clubhouses were built for the entertainment of these new pilots, hosting fashionable soirées that regularly attracted the cream of Paris society. Maryse Bastié opened her flying school, alongside Sens de l'Air ('airmanship') and the Forlex-Mauboussin school, to mention only the most prestigious. The air force also trained its pilots at Orly. With the training came the first plane hire companies like Potez Aero Service and Farman Air Service.

At the outbreak of war in 1939, the facilities of the aerodrome were requisitioned by the government. It was from the Orly military base that Antoine de Saint-Exupéry and his navigator took off on 23 May 1940 in a Bloch MB174 on a photo-reconnaissance mission. The writer gives an account of this flight in *Pilote de Guerre*, published in the United States under the title *Flight to Arras*. On 3 June 1940, the site was bombed by the Germans. It was seriously damaged, but the big airship hangars were untouched. Several civil aircraft outside the hangars were destroyed. Under the Occupation, the Luftwaffe laid down two hard-surfaced runways: one 1,550m long in the direction of the prevailing east-west winds, the other north-south, 1,860m long. A large number of taxiways were also laid down. The aerodrome was extended to the east as far as the first houses in Athis Mons. The field was occupied by several fighter squadrons, flying the Messerschmitt Bf 109 E and the Junkers Ju 88A. From Orly they carried out night attacks on London and southern England.

The riposte from the 8th Air Force in May and June 1944 was overwhelming. The airship hangars were destroyed, and the control tower built by the Germans was partly destroyed. On 22 August 1944, the first American planes landed at Orly, P47s of the 313th Tactical Fighter Squadron. The Paris site was a necessary stop-over for the American pilots before moving on to Laon in the Aisne. The bomb craters resulting from the allied bombing were filled in the following day by American military engineers. The runways were repaired, reinforced and extended, and aids to navigation for landing in poor light were installed. Damaged buildings were rebuilt and enlarged to house the staff of Air Transport Command, including living quarters, a mess, a chapel, a cinema and grocery stores. A temporary wood-built airport terminal was built to receive pilots and air traffic controllers en route to the Middle and Far East. This included an arrivals lounge, a departures lounge, a transit lounge and several shops. There was a bar to provide refreshments for passengers.

One year after the end of the Second World War, the Orly site and its installations were officially returned to France, handed over by Colonel Smith to Commandant Crémont, the future head of Orly, in the presence of Max Hymans, the new secretary general for civil and commercial aviation. —

The Orly American base in November 1918.

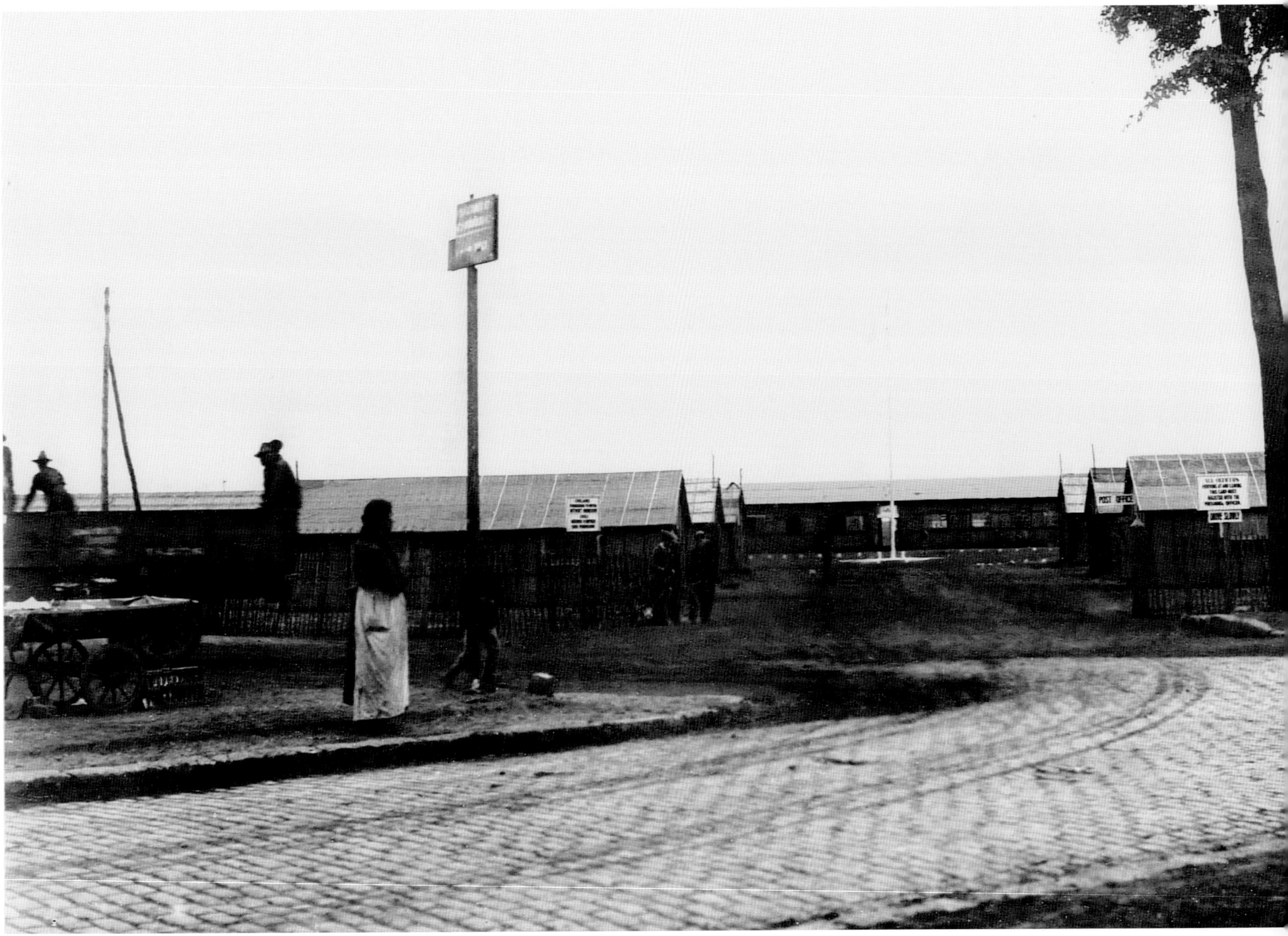
POST OFFICE
DRIVE SLOWLY

Left: The Orly American base in November 1918.

Above: Port Aviation's signal tower in 1909.

INSTALLING MOTOR IN BREGUET PLANE

Fitting the motor in a Breguet plane at the Orly American base in November 1918.

A plane at the Orly American base in November 1918.

2 Champ d'Aviation d'ORLY - VILLENEUVE-LE-ROI - Hangar à dirigeable, longueur 100 m., hauteur 58 m.

Above: Postcard showing the Orly hangars in the 1920s (Orly flying field).

Opposite page: Zodiac E9 in front of the Orly hangars, end of the 1920s.

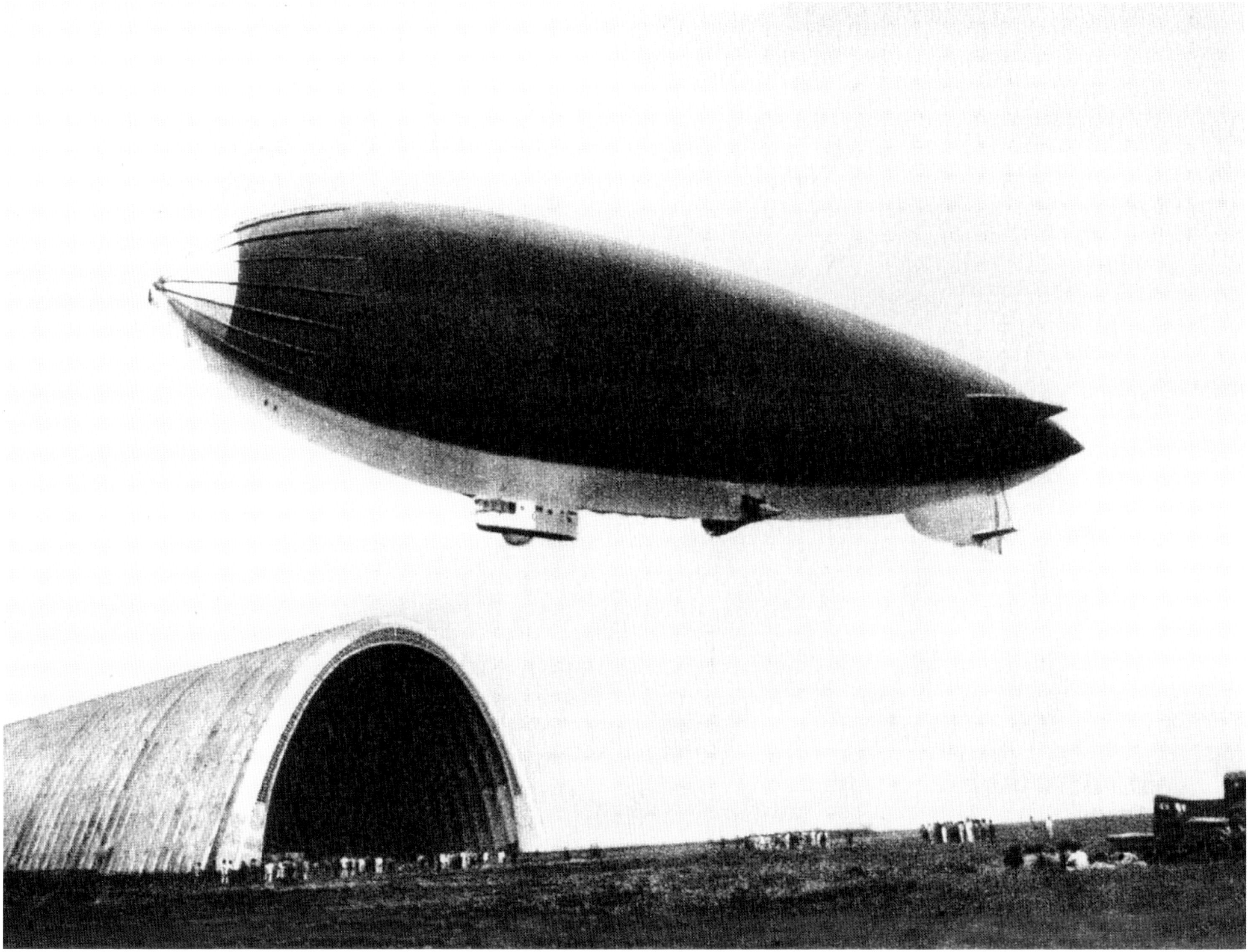

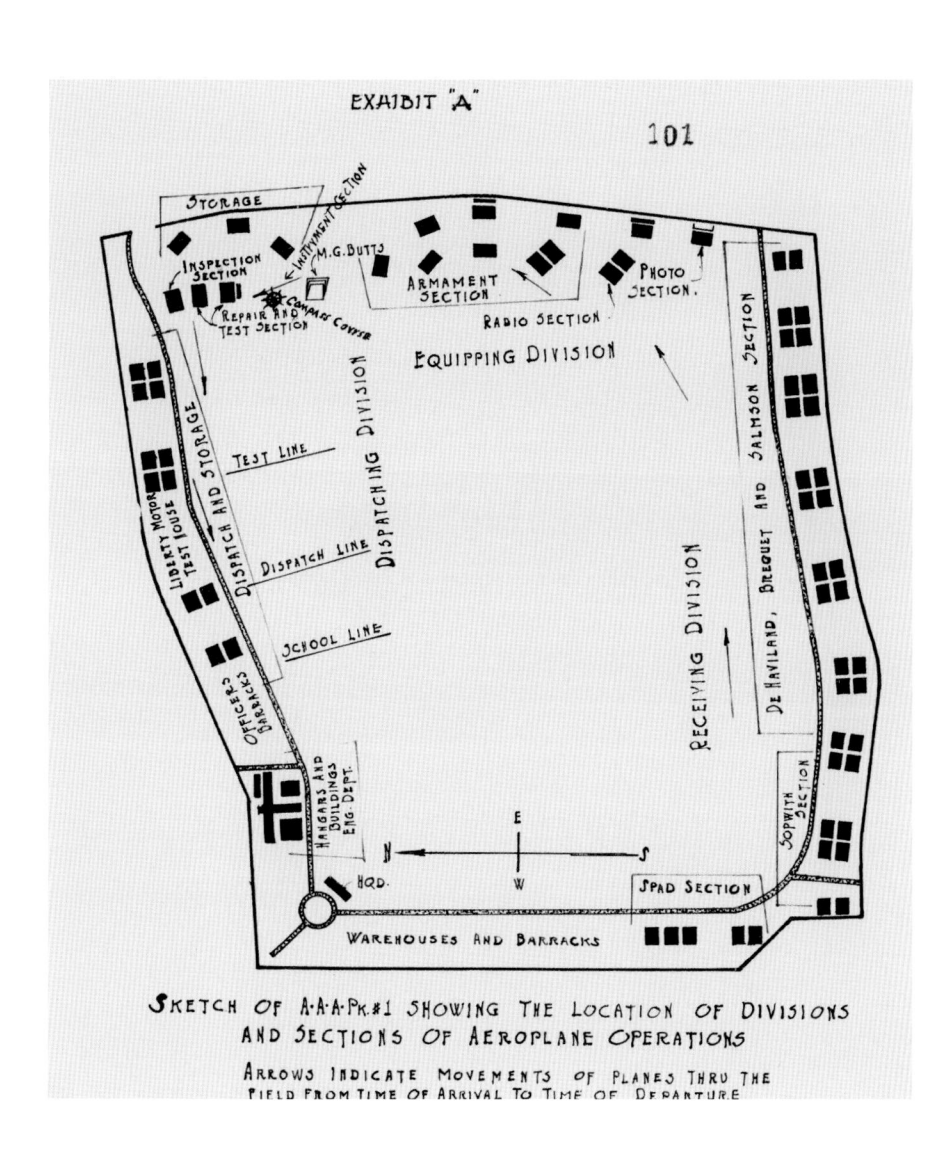

Above left: Plan of the installation drawn by the works manager, probably Eli Baxter Springs, sergeant major in the Second Mechanical Air Service Regiment, Sixth Company under the command of Captain Ambler.

Above right: Aerial view of the Orly American base in 1918.

Above left: List of air taxi fares in 1921.

Above right: Publicity poster for "night flights over Paris", 1920s.

Above: Orly flying field, showing entrance to the air marine storage facility.

Opposite page: Airship hangars.

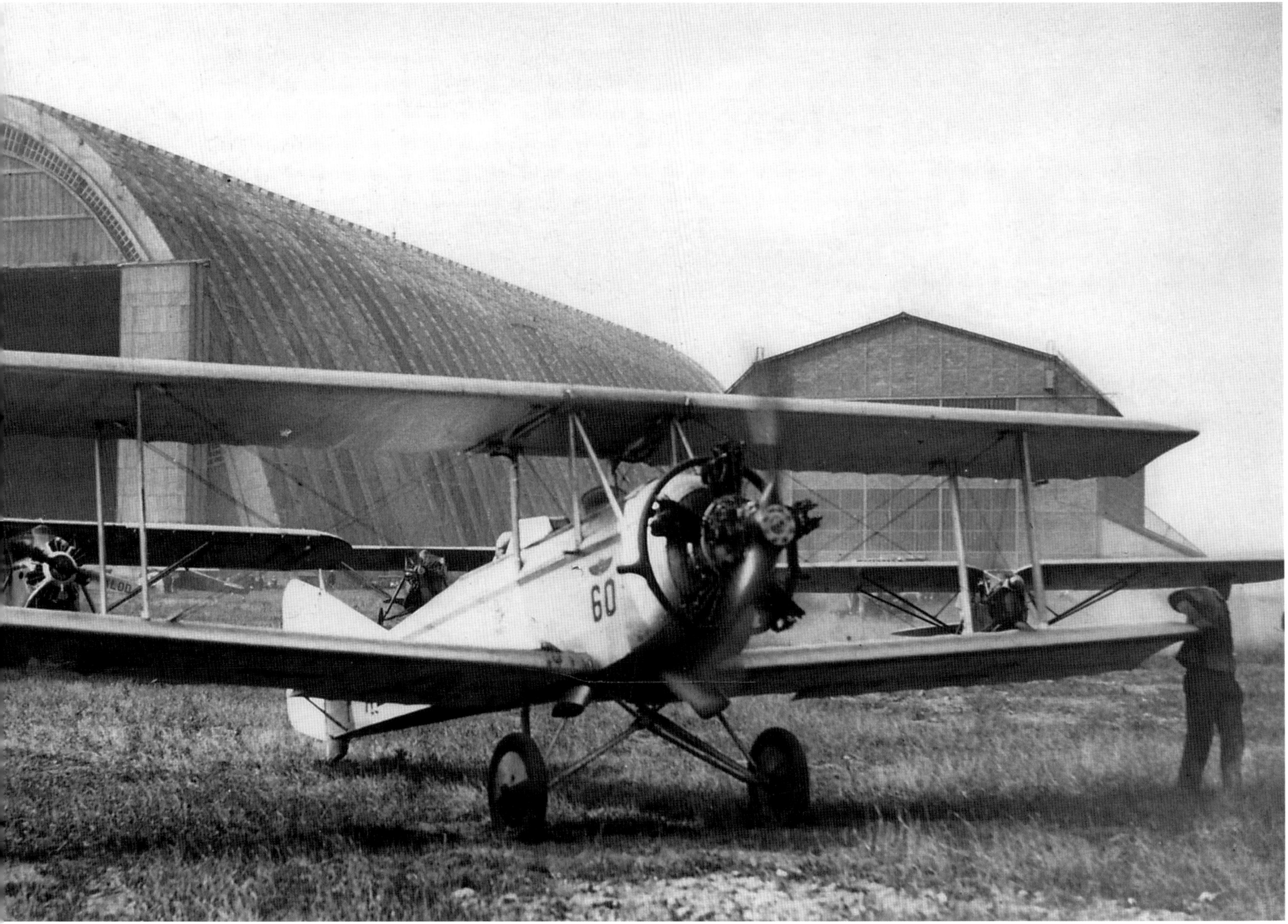
60

The Richard Hangars in the 1920s.

Flying display in front of the Freyssinet Hangars, 1920s.

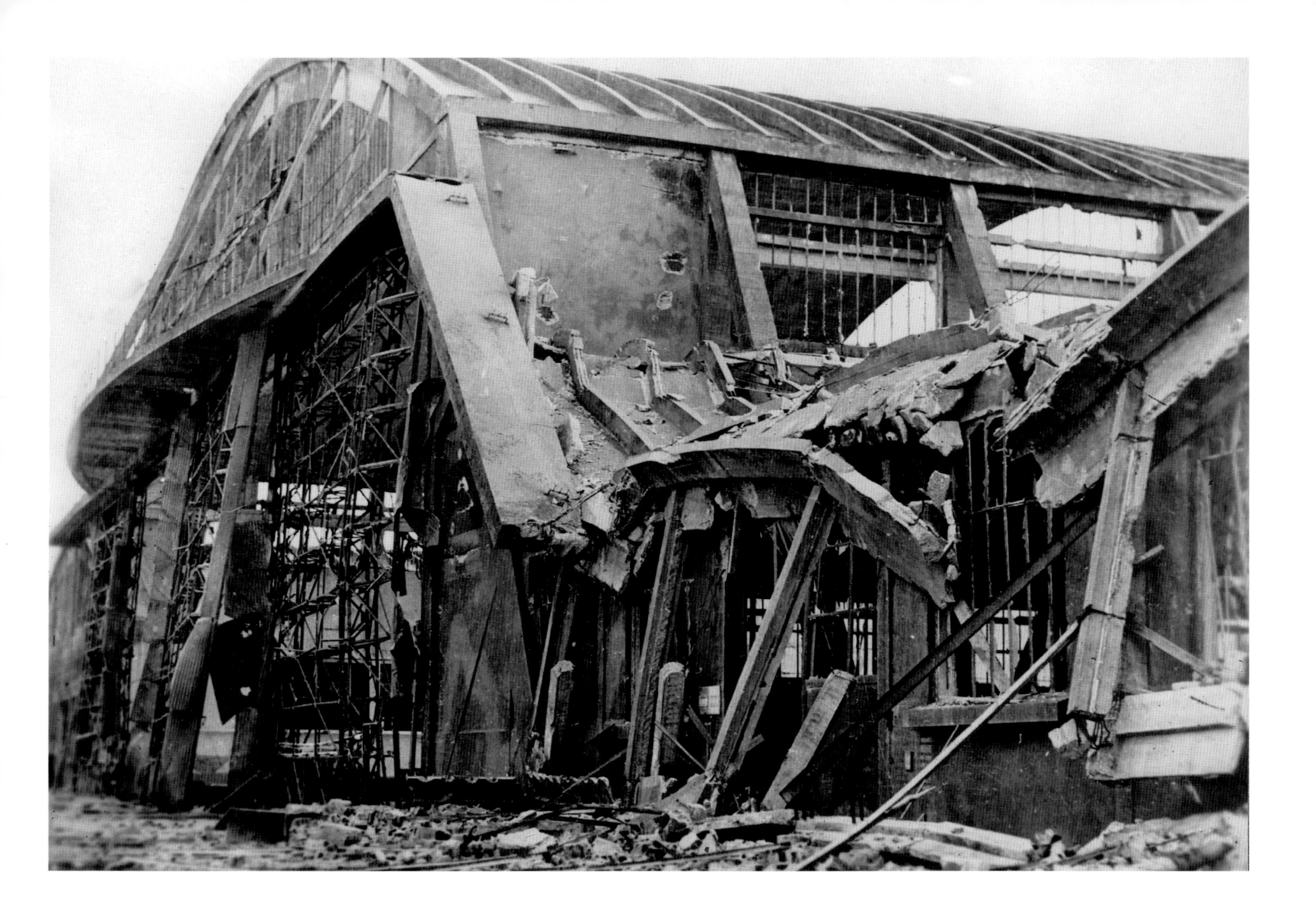

Hangars destroyed in the War, August 1945.

Top left: Orly occupied by the Germans. The plane is a Ju 88A of the KG51 battle wing.

Above left: German guard in front of the hangars.

Above right: German control tower.

Aerial view of Orly in the 1940s.

The aftermath of German bombing: a Potez 63-11 between two Breguet 27s.

COMMERCIAL AVIATION TAKES OFF

1945-1961

IT WAS NOVEMBER 1944, BEFORE THE WAR HAD ENDED.

Alain Bozel, secretary general of the ministry for War, proposed an airports authority, charged with the management of airports and aerodromes within a 50 kilometer radius of Paris. The decision was finally ratified a year later, on 24 October 1945, by General de Gaulle, with the statutory creation of the autonomous public body, Aéroports de Paris (ADP). Managed by an administrative council of 22 members, this new public body would set about creating a Parisian airport. It would meanwhile take charge of some 15 other airports, among them Le Bourget, Pontoise, Toussus le Noble, Saint Cyr l'École, Lognes, Chavenay and Guyancourt. Orly Airport now had the wind behind it. Already the Germans had bequeathed two concrete runways, one with an east-west orientation 1,825m long, the other north-south, 1,560m long. Le Bourget only had one. One year after the end of the Second World War on 7 November 1946, Orly Airport and its installations were officially returned to France.

"Among the air ministry's projects, Orly will become one of the biggest airports in Europe. Here runways more than 3.5km long will make blind landings possible. Plans include a vast hotel, a post office and a rail link with the Gare d'Orsay," explained a report sent to General de Gaulle. Thanks to two concrete runways and the temporary air terminal built by the Americans, transatlantic connections were quickly re-established. It was also at this time that the concept of *droits de trafic* emerged. A first agreement was signed between France and the United States. The American operators would serve the East Indies via Orly, and the Orient via Marseille. For their part, the French operators, such as Air France, were authorized to open routes to New York, Boston and Washington. In 1947, the Chicago Convention set out the regulatory framework for these bilateral agreements. In the first instance, the operation of these routes was handled by military crews in Douglas C-54s under the command of Air Traffic Control (ATC). These military pilots had considerable experience of long overseas flights. Before the Americans left, North Atlantic crossings departed every 19 minutes, amounting to more than 9,000 flights in total between 1942 and 1944.

Routes to Europe were by stages taken over by the American companies Pan Am, TWA and American Airlines. The fall of Japan in August 1945 progressively freed the American personnel of companies that had been requisitioned.

These companies would take advantage of the surplus aircraft that the American army was now selling off cheap – and they were in no way obliged to return the Douglas DC3s and DC4s that they had borrowed. This gave the civil American fleet a considerable advantage over the competition. The French government protested, and there were protracted negotiations between Paris and Washington to find a fair solution.

French air transport was merged as one body in February 1945 under the name Réseau des Lignes Aériennes Françaises (RLAF). Several months later, French civil aviation was nationalized. The formerly private company Air France was taken over by the state and placed in charge of the total French flight network. Like its American competitors, Air France gathered up many craft from the military, assembling a large fleet of DC3s, DC4s and the Bloch SE161 Languedoc, ancestor of Dassault aircraft. France could at last spread its wings. Air France opened many routes out of Orly with connections along the way, to New York, Santiago in Chili, Rio, Casablanca, Cairo and Saigon. To maintain space between flights and for aircraft security, the training of air traffic controllers commenced. But in the time before the creation of the École Nationale de l'Aviation Civile (ENAC), the supervision of air traffic was entrusted to American controllers.

The DC3s and DC4s were progressively replaced by a much more modern plane, more powerful and most notably the first to have a pressurized cabin. This was the Constellation from American constructor Lockheed, and it was this aircraft that brought commercial aviation into the era of regular transatlantic flights. On 6 February 1946, a TWA Constellation *Star of Paris* flew from New York via Gander in Newfoundland and Shannon in Ireland to land at Orly after a flight of 15 hours and 58 minutes at a speed of more than 450kph with 36 passengers on board. The plane made its return journey to the United States the same evening. The Constellation was a most elegant plane that quickly became the symbol of a certain modern style with a touch of luxury.

Then Air France achieved a World First. In October 1947, it launched a special service between Orly and New York with a Constellation fitted with 11 couchettes. Air France was universally recognized for the luxury of its services, such as the *Épicurien* service to London and the *Parisien-Spécial* to New York. For the first time, the company would serve hot meals on its long-haul flights. Orly needed places along the way for the production of these meals, and transatlantic collaboration increased accordingly.

With traffic on the increase, new airport facilities were needed. The temporary wooden terminal building that the Americans built at the end of the War was no longer enough. Flight centre management put in place a special planning service charged with improving airport infrastructure, and a mission hurried over to the United States. They came back with a proposal for ten tangential runways, two of them 3,000m long and 100m wide. Cost was estimated at 26 million francs, much too high. Eventually this plan was abandoned in favor of a single landing runway parallel to the existing east-west runway that could be used when visibility was bad. At the end of 1947, the 2,100m long Runway 3 was officially opened. The wooden structures were demolished to make way for a building in solid masonry, the North Terminal, opened in 1948. But it was plain that this was a provisional solution, considering future traffic predictions and the risk of saturation. The navy had meanwhile resumed its pre-War activity on the site despite the destruction of the two airship hangars in the course of the War. Up until 1966 when France quit NATO, it maintained substantial activity at the south Paris airport. The Americans meanwhile kept a small part of their base for the management of flight connections and the handling of VIP passengers.

Traffic increased by more than 15% each year. In 1948, Orly received 215,000 passengers, compared with 360,000 at Le Bourget. The same year, parliament approved the new nationalized status of Air France, making it a *compagnie nationale, société d'économie mixte, régie par le Code de l'Aviation Civile*. President of the board of directors was Max Hymans.

Aviation made considerable progress and air travel continued to close the distances between continents.

In October 1948, Louis Couhé, former director of the Compagnie Générale Transatlantique, became president of the board of Aéroports de Paris. The contest between Orly in the south and Le Bourget in the north had begun.

For the present, Air France maintained its domestic connections, with international flights being handled out of Orly. Then everything moved very quickly. In 1952, Orly passengers passed the million mark – a record – double the figure for Le Bourget, which was constrained by the pace of surrounding urban development. This time, Air France decided to move all of its activities to the south Paris airport. By way of compensation, the capital's northern airport won back the international air show (Salon International de l'Aéronautique) and the organization of air shows in general. For the 20th edition of the Salon du Bourget in 1953, Air France organized a short transfer between the two airports, giving the company's guests the chance to compare the qualities of the two facilities.

By stages, Orly's facilities improved. In 1953, the first radar was installed. The following year, a new control tower was built, along with a regional control centre, these new features inaugurated by transport minister Jacques Chaban-Delmas. In 1957, a VOR (VHF omni-directional range measuring system) was installed to make the approach to the airport more exact, which was welcomed by residents who were beginning to complain about aircraft noise. Airport passenger tax was also introduced in 1954, fixed by an order dated 11 October at 400 francs for European and North African destinations, 1,200 francs for other continents.

The planes were now progressively bigger and heavier, and the structure of the runways had to be reinforced. The area of the airport rose from 800 to 1,600 hectares. The Paray Vieille Poste farm and its outbuildings were removed. New access roads were required for the public, and visitor parking was needed. An expressway was built to connect the airport to the RN7 highway. Eventually it would be connected to the future Autoroute du Soleil freeway which came into service in 1960. The French now discovered the pleasures of the car and traffic jams.

To allow the westward lengthening of the main runway to 3,300m and the building of a new terminal, it was decided to run the RN7 highway underground.

On 14 August 1954, a new South Terminal was opened. This was the first substantial project undertaken by Aéroports de Paris (ADP). For the first time, the flow of passenger traffic was split between arrivals and departures.

The RN7 road tunnel was inaugurated in November 1959, several months before the opening of the A6 freeway. Relatively noisy jet planes by stages replaced propeller aircraft. Alongside the Constellations appeared the first Boeing 707 Intercontinentals, the Caravelles and DC8s.

With the arrival of these new planes, a *Bureau des riverains* (office to serve local residents) was put in place. Aircraft routes were chosen to minimize the disturbance to communities bordering the airport. To assist the approach of planes in fog, new systems were trialed, and jet engines were installed on the ground to clear fog from the runway (this was before the effect of the petrol crisis was felt).

Two first hangars, N1 and N2, were built for aircraft maintenance. They were huge, nearly 19,000m², and nearly 900 tons of steel were required to build them. Next came N5 and N6, raising the total floor area to 35,000m². Each door ran on huge rails and weighed nearly 30 tons. This was at the time the biggest cantilevered hangar in the world. With the arrival of jet planes came hangars N7 and N8. A thermo-electric power plant was installed as insurance against power cuts.

Meanwhile a new company named Air Inter was formed to serve internal routes. The first flight was 16 March 1958 between Strasbourg and Paris. Objectives at the outset were very ambitious, shareholders Air France and SNCF rail expecting to operate some twenty routes. Their hopes were

Air France Douglas DC4 refueling in front of the North Terminal (opened in 1948). The terminal was located on the site of the present gendarmerie in the freight area.

Official opening ceremony by the French president, General de Gaulle, on 24 February 1961.

quickly dashed, due to lack of promotion and a discouraging ticket price. Air Inter only really took off in 1960, under the leadership of Admiral Paul Hébrard, a former pilot and trailblazer for the Air France Far East network. He drove the campaign to draw local groups and chambers of commerce into the development of the network. Thanks to the general availability of planes for charter, DC3s, DC4s and Lockheed Constellations, the activities of Air Inter took off again.

> **France was enjoying its period of prosperity known as the *Trente Glorieuses*. The shadow of General de Gaulle soared over French politics, and modernity and progress were now society's prevailing values.**

The extension of the Orly site was approved, and architect Henri Vicariot was charged with the construction of a new South Terminal. The planning of this terminal took ten years. Building took just four (1957-1961) and employed 1,200 workmen. The budget was set at 50 million francs in the money of those times.

Plain materials were used, leaving scope for future expansion that would not spoil the architectural style. The terminal was planned on six levels, and fitted out to the very latest standards – a building designed to evolve. Henri Vicariot made considerable use of stainless steel, aluminum and enameled glass, a modernist style inspired by buildings in the United States. The curtain wall construction here was the first to appear in France. It gave an unbeatable view over the activity of the airport and gave the traveler a powerful impression of space. It seemed you could reach out and touch the planes. The atmosphere of the building was luminous and airy, and the great hall on the first floor was bigger than anything seen in public buildings at the time. The scale of the building was monumental, like an enormous metal slab, 200m long, 70m deep, with an area of 13,000m^2.

The erection of the metal framework and superstructures started in 1958. The following year saw the mounting of the facades, the installation of vertical and horizontal ducting and then in 1960 the fitting-out of the interiors. The South Terminal was opened on 24 January 1961 by General de Gaulle, after three and a half years of work. Before an audience of VIPs, he saluted the work of Henri Vicariot: "If ever a work justified the pride of those who built it, with their brains and with their hands, it is certainly the work that we see here, where sky meets earth. We have added something to the human relationships of the present and the future." A stamp depicting the airport was issued to mark the event. The terminal was planned to handle as many as six million passengers a year – Orly was where commercial mass transport first took off.

Arrivals were processed on the eastern side, departures at the western end. Passengers took escalators to the departure lounges on the first floor. Luggage moved around on conveyor belts, which was a great novelty. Passenger information was broadcast throughout the terminal in several languages. The processing of passengers for international flights took place on the first floor, which had a customs area.

> **For the modest sum of 50 old francs, you could watch the coming and going of planes from the open-air terraces. Caravelles and Boeing 707s brought smiles to the faces of curious onlookers.**

The first direct flights from Paris to New York took off from Orly. The luxury boutiques, the cinema, the terraces, the bars and restaurants made Orly a major centre of attraction for visitors.

It was stylish for stars to be photographed here. Orly South Terminal was much more than a simple travel facility. People went to Orly to watch an airliner, to admire the latest wonders of technology. Orly South quickly became famous as an emblem of French excellence and the modern style of the 'sixties. —

Above: Air France Douglas DC3 in front of the first wood-built terminal, photo 1952-1953.

Right: A Comet on the ground in 1953.

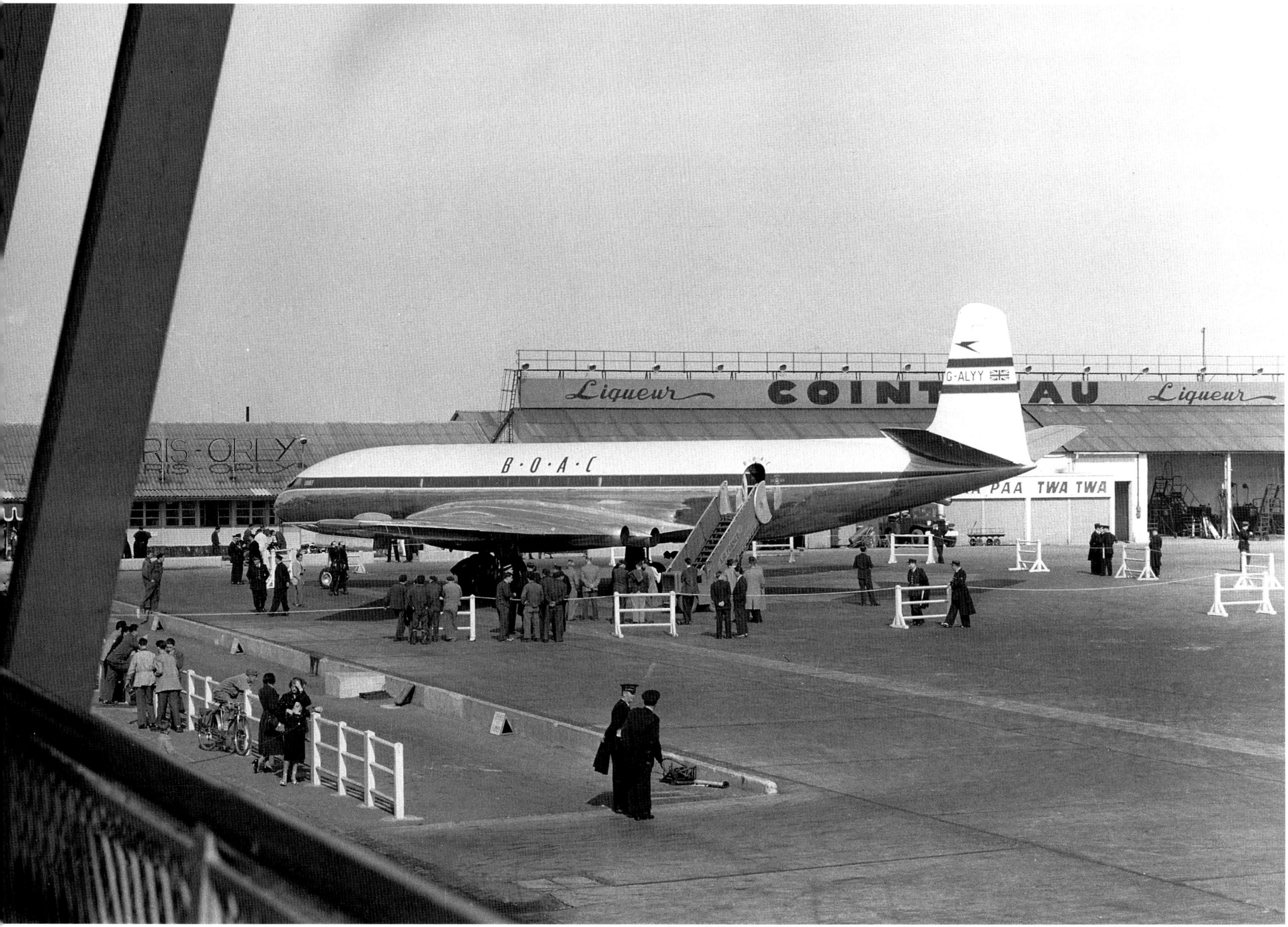
Liqueur
COINT
AU
Liqueur
B·O·A·C
G-ALYY
PAA TWA TWA

Guided tour of Orly by bus, passing the control tower, 2 March 1954.

School pupils on a guided visit in 1952.

TWA Constellation in front of the North Terminal in 1952.

The terraces of the first South Terminal in 1956/1958.

THE FIRST FLIGHT FROM ORLY TO NEW YORK

On 6 February 1946, Orly received its first regular flight of the post-War period. A TWA Constellation from New York landed at the Paris airport. The flight had taken more than 20 hours. This first commercial connection across the Atlantic was the beginning of the era of regular transatlantic flights. Several months later, Air France introduced its *Ruban Etoilé* route, the name given to the first commercial connection between Paris and New York. On 23 June 1946, at 19.00h, the DC4 *Ciel Île-de-France* left Orly to land at La Guardia 23 hours and 45 minutes later – an average speed of 305kph. There were 33 passengers on board, and the flight went without a hitch. The plane stopped off at Shannon in Ireland, then Gander in Newfoundland. On arrival in New York, the airhostess presented president Harry Truman's wife with a bouquet of Picardy roses fresh from Paris.

In September 1949, Air France introduced the first in-flight hot meals, supplied by the Orly hotel service. Flourishing relationships between France and the United States encouraged the national carrier to increase its flights to this destination. Two flights a week in 1946 increased to one per day in 1954. The transatlantic connection used the Lockheed Constellation L049, followed by the Super Constellation L1049. The "Paris Special" service was introduced, with beds, private cabins and a gastronomic menu. Eight private cabins were fitted, converted at night by the air stewards to double beds, and there were 16 armchair couchettes – the most luxurious facilities ever installed in an aircraft. The crew was specially trained for this prestige service.

For nearly ten years, this luxurious package switched between DC3 and DC4, and the journey time was cut to 17 hours. In 1958 the time was faster still, when Pan Am introduced its Boeing 707 service between New York and Orly. In 1960, it was the same plane that took to the route in the colors of Air France. It was baptized *Château de Versailles* and carried 120 passengers. From Orly, it flew to Idlewild Airport – renamed Kennedy Airport in 1963 – and the journey time was now down to eight hours and 15 minutes.

Opposite page: Air France Douglas DC4 refueling in 1952.

Left: Douglas DC4 in front of the North Terminal in 1952.

45

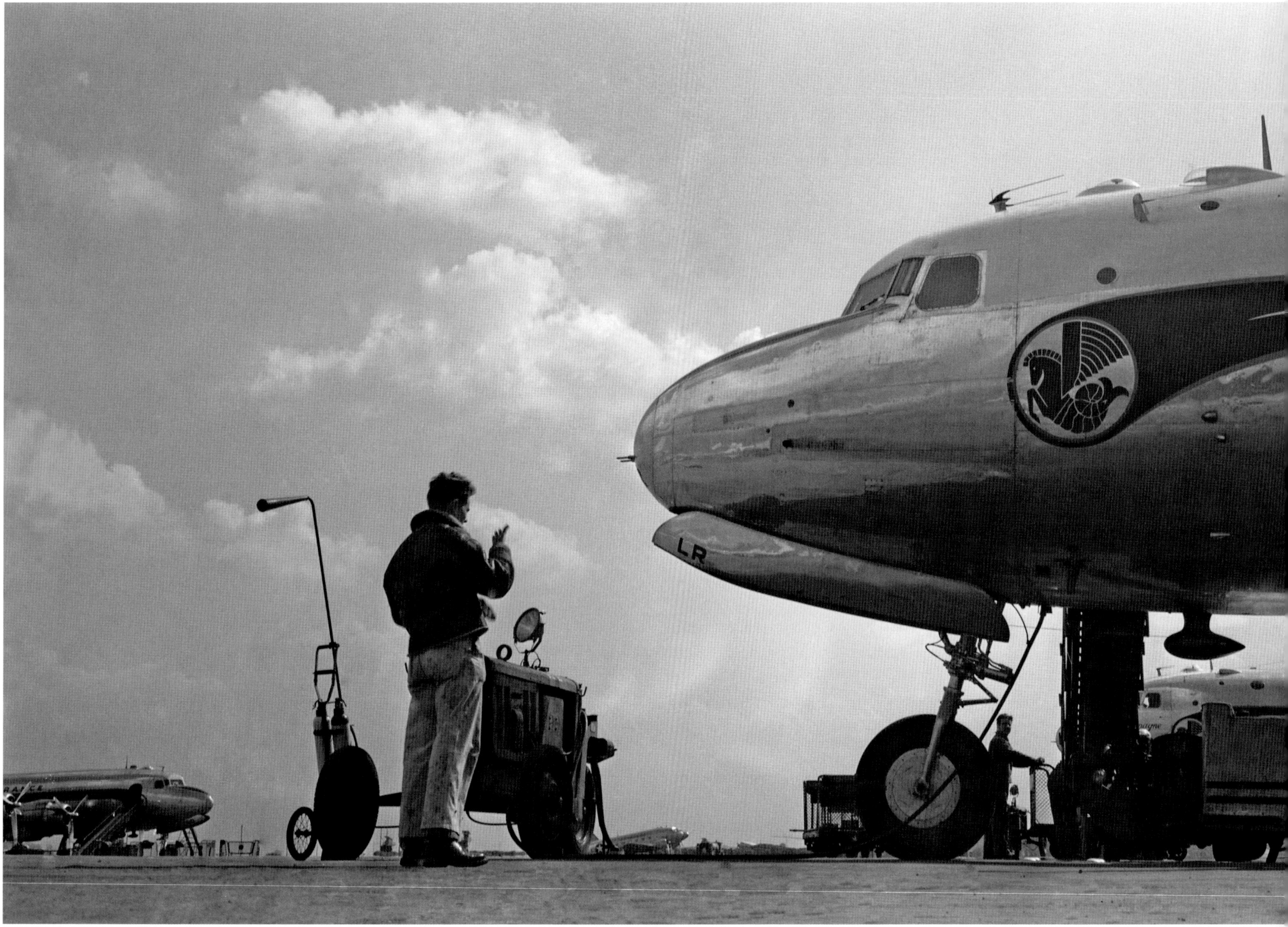
LR

Opposite page: Air France Constellation in 1954.

Above: TAI (Transports Aériens Intercontinentaux) Douglas DC4 in 1952.

First South Terminal in 1956.

Constellations on the tarmac in 1954.

Passengers in the temporary South Terminal, 23 October 1956.

Above right: Interior of the temporary South Terminal in 1955.

Opposite page: Station staff in ADP uniform in 1958.

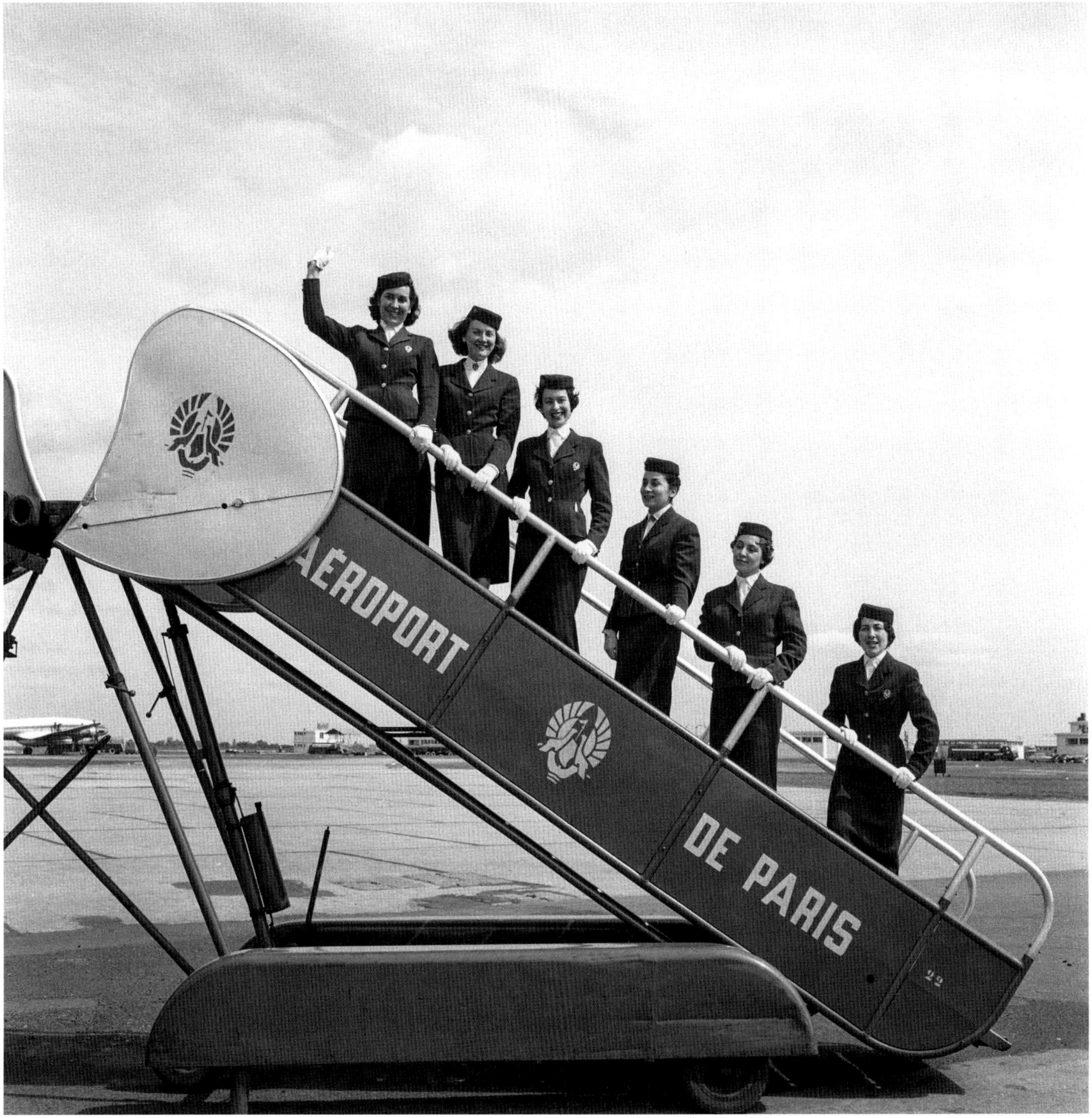
AÉROPORT
DE PARIS

The first South Terminal in 1956.

First South Terminal with Dunlop footbridge in 1955.

A HISTORIC AND STRATEGIC PARTNERSHIP LINKS PARIS-ORLY TO AIR FRANCE-KLM. OUR COMPANIES ARE THEREFORE INTIMATELY INVOLVED IN THE FUTURE OF THIS AIRPORT, AND WE EXPECT TO REINFORCE THIS COLLABORATION IN THE COMING YEARS.

Jean-Marc Janaillac, president and CEO
of Air France-KLM

Opposite page: Air France Constellation in 1955.

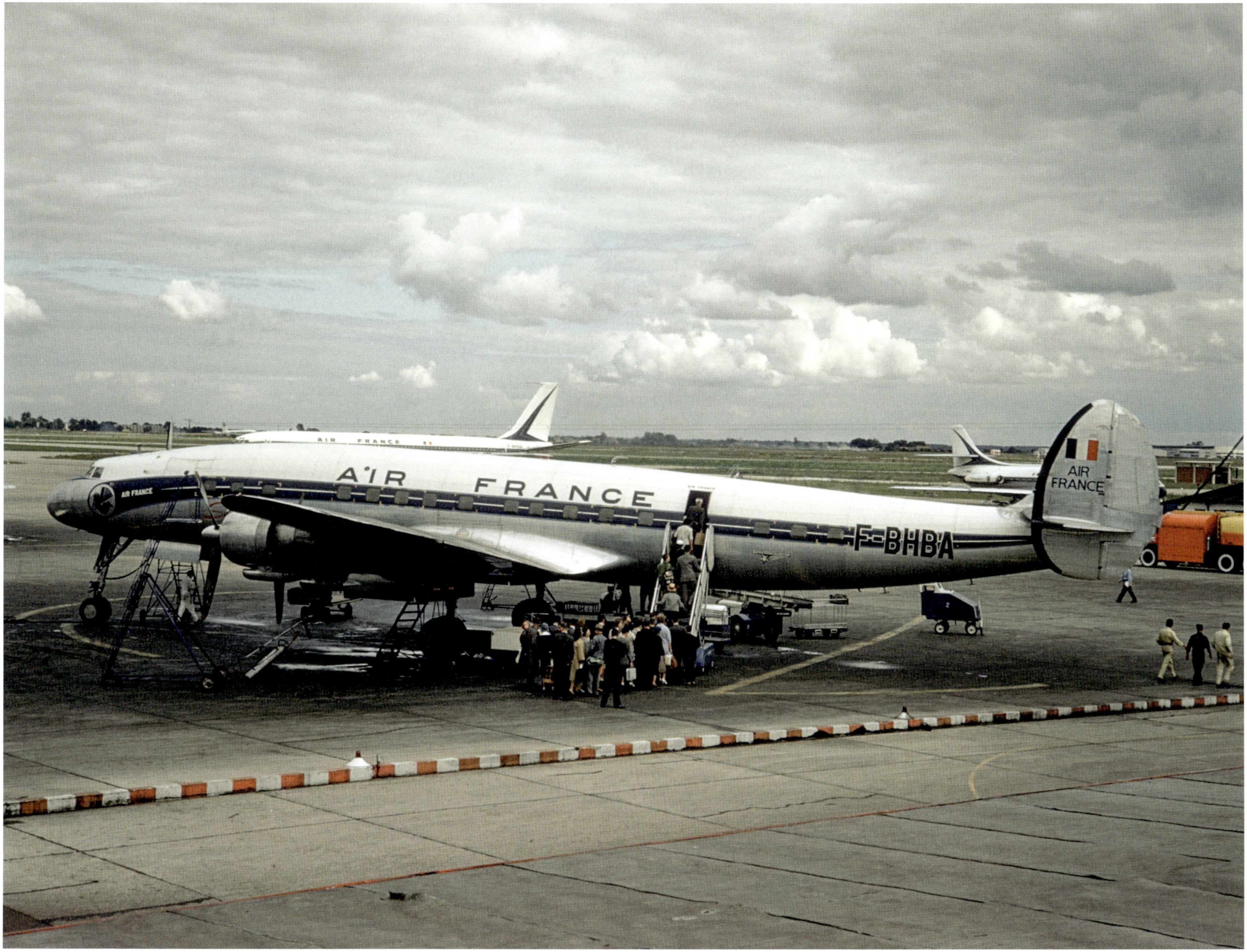
AIR FRANCE
F-BHBA
AIR
FRANCE

Managing flight connections in 1958.

Air traffic controllers in 1959.

The control tower radar screen.

Above: Runway agents with tractors in front of the terminal in 1958.

Opposite page: Passengers disembarking from a Caravelle in 1958.

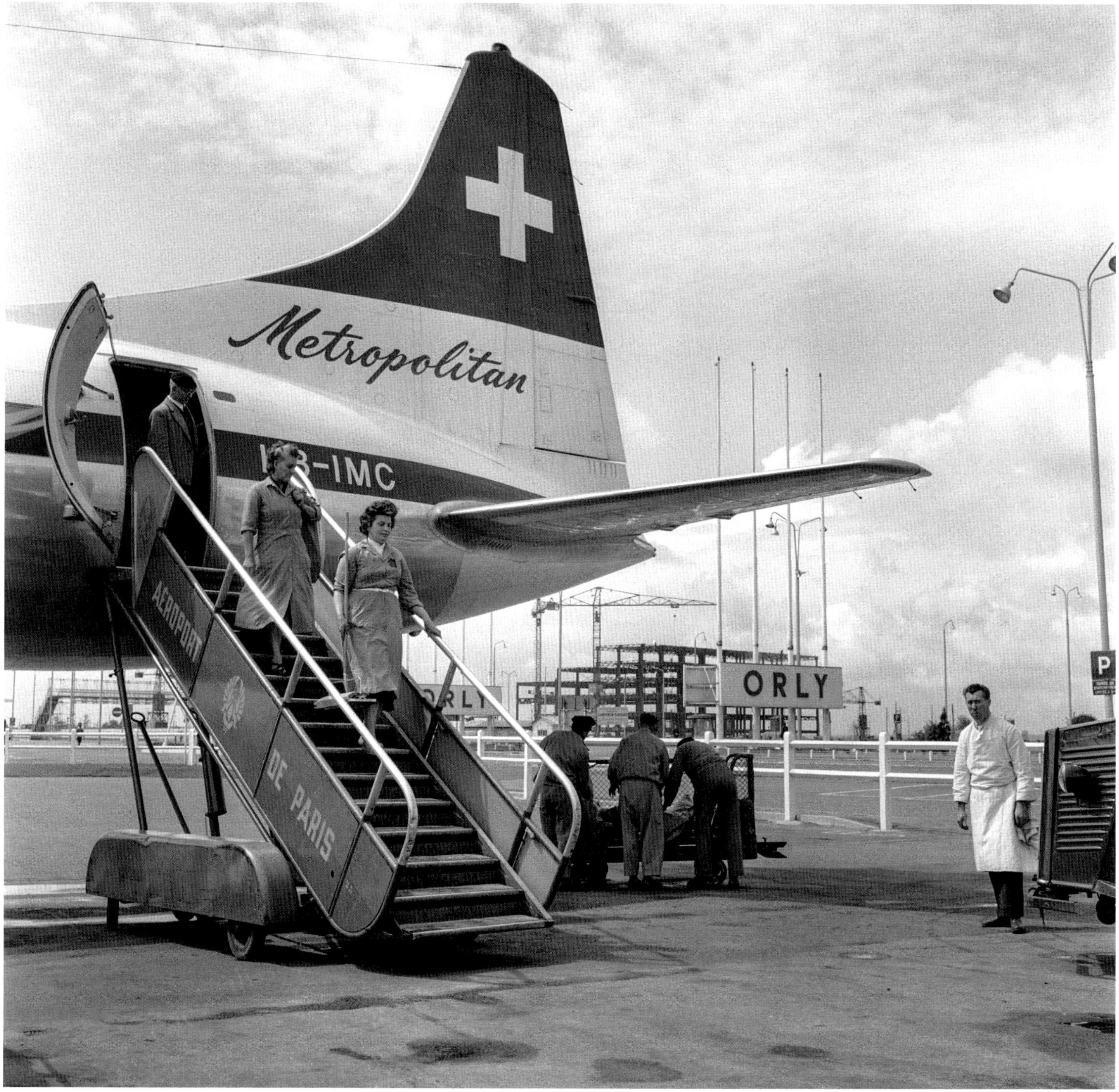
Metropolitan
-IMC
AEROPORT DE PARIS
ORLY
ORLY
P

HENRI VICARIOT
MASTER OF AIRPORT DESIGN

Henri Vicariot designed the huge solar oven at Font Romeu, the RER station at La Défense, and many bridges and public buildings in France and overseas. But he is above all noted for Orly South Terminal, his masterpiece. For nearly ten years, this civil engineer and graduate of the Beaux Arts was the master in charge of the construction of the South Terminal. He began his career as an engineering officer and, when fighting ended in 1940, he switched course and enrolled in the Paris Institut d'Urbanisme (town planning school). He studied architecture, then also studied at the École des Ponts et Chaussées (school of bridge and roadway design) where he finished top of his class in 1947.

Henri Vicariot was recruited to the air-base management department of the Secrétariat Général à l'Aviation Civile et Commerciale (SGACC). Then he was attached to Aéroports de Paris (ADP) which would be the focus of his whole architectural career. He rebuilt aircraft maintenance hangars and offices, and renovated the old control tower. Then the rapid development of air traffic at the end of the War gave him the chance to demonstrate his talent as a creator of new buildings. The government had grand plans. Orly would become Europe's premier airport, with a modern architectural style that expressed the renewal of France. Two buildings symbolized this renewal: the Maison de la Radio built in the period 1956-1963; and the Orly South Terminal.

Vicariot favored a style of architecture that was sober, classical and lasting, free of the influence of passing trends. A visit to the United States proved decisive. Impressed by the transparency of American facades, he was the first in France to build with curtain walls and use new materials such as enameled glass, stainless steel and anodized aluminum – materials well represented in the Orly terminals. His American experience also introduced him to the techniques of very complete and detailed design planning, to avoid risks and surprises in the course of construction. A devotee of interior design, he put together multi-disciplinary teams of architects, engineers and interior designers, combining all of the disciplines that modern construction might require. With his range of perspectives and overall project vision, Vicariot developed a total approach to airport design, the way you plan and design a town.

The South Terminal was opened on 24 January 1961 by General de Gaulle. Traffic continued to grow and Henri Vicariot was very soon at work on a second terminal. The construction of Orly West started in 1967, Henri Vicariot working in collaboration with three other architects. The terminal opened on 24 February 1971. Being an all-round engineer, he also designed a series of bridges to allow roads to pass under the runways. Vicariot was an internationally recognized specialist in the design of airports, who developed his know-how in France and many countries throughout the world. The airports of Clermont Ferrand, Toulouse and Nice are owed to him, as are the airports of Beyrouth, Damascus, Lisbon and Istanbul.

Opposite page: Henri Vicariot in 1961.

Left: The metal structure of the South Terminal construction site in 1959.

Below: Construction of the control tower in 1965.

Bottom: Several stages in the evolution of the control tower project, drawn by Henri Vicariot.

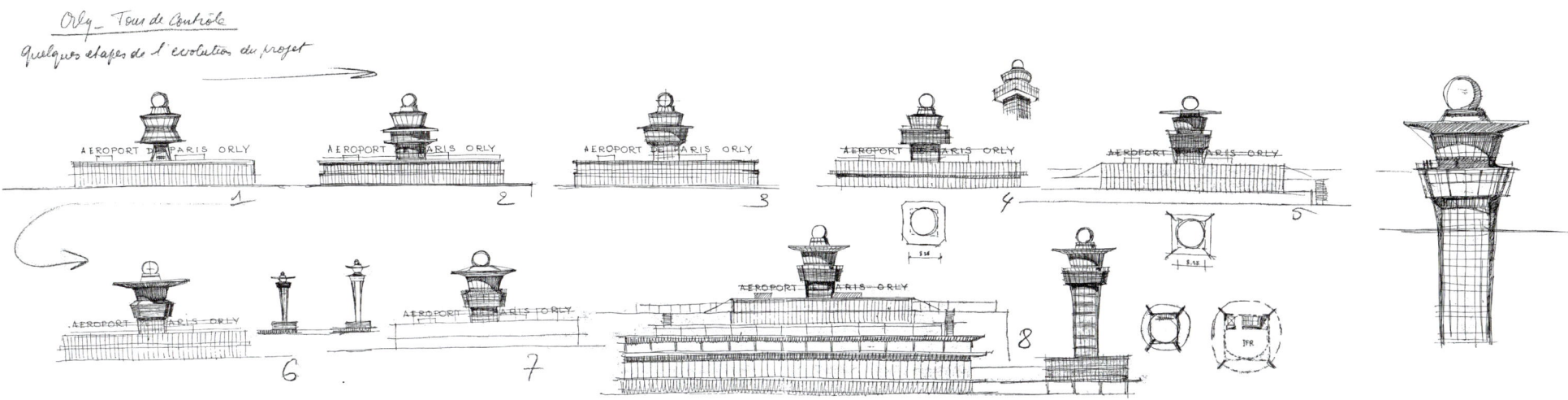

Above: South Terminal construction site in 1959.

Right: South Terminal site and the re-routing of the N7 highway.

62

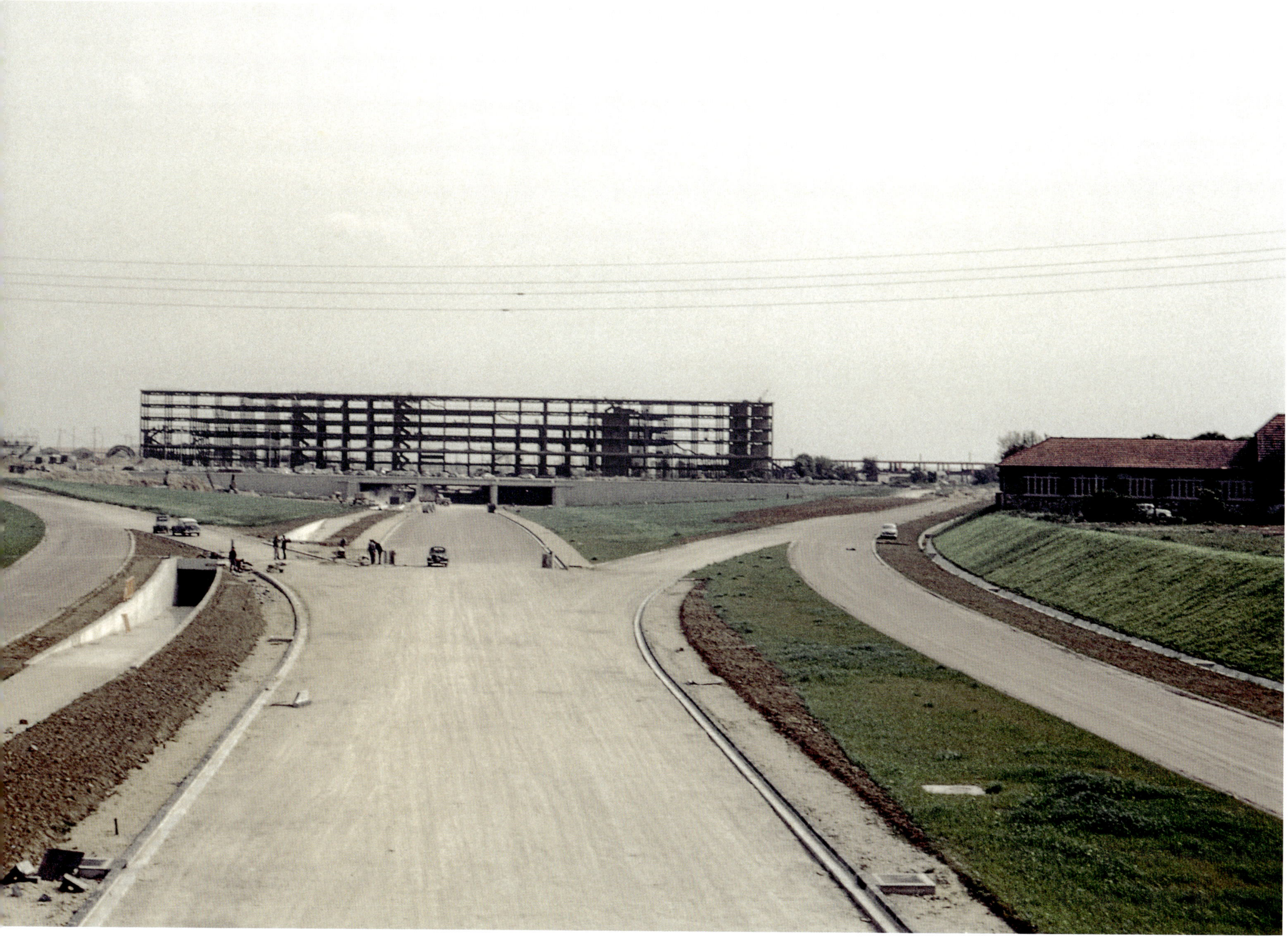

Above: Interior of the original control tower in 1955.

Opposite page: Caravelle on the tarmac in front of the South Terminal, 1962.

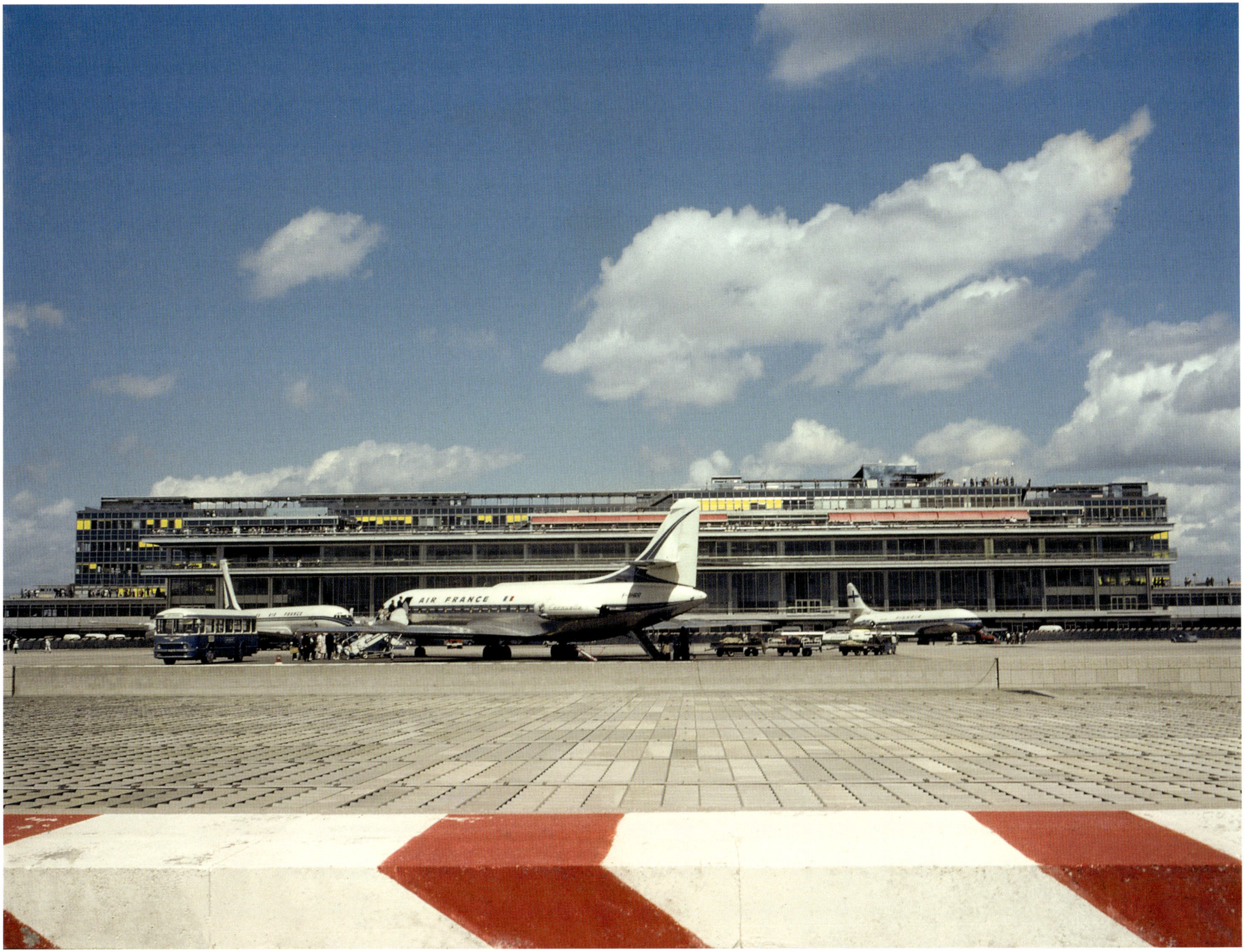
AIR FRANCE

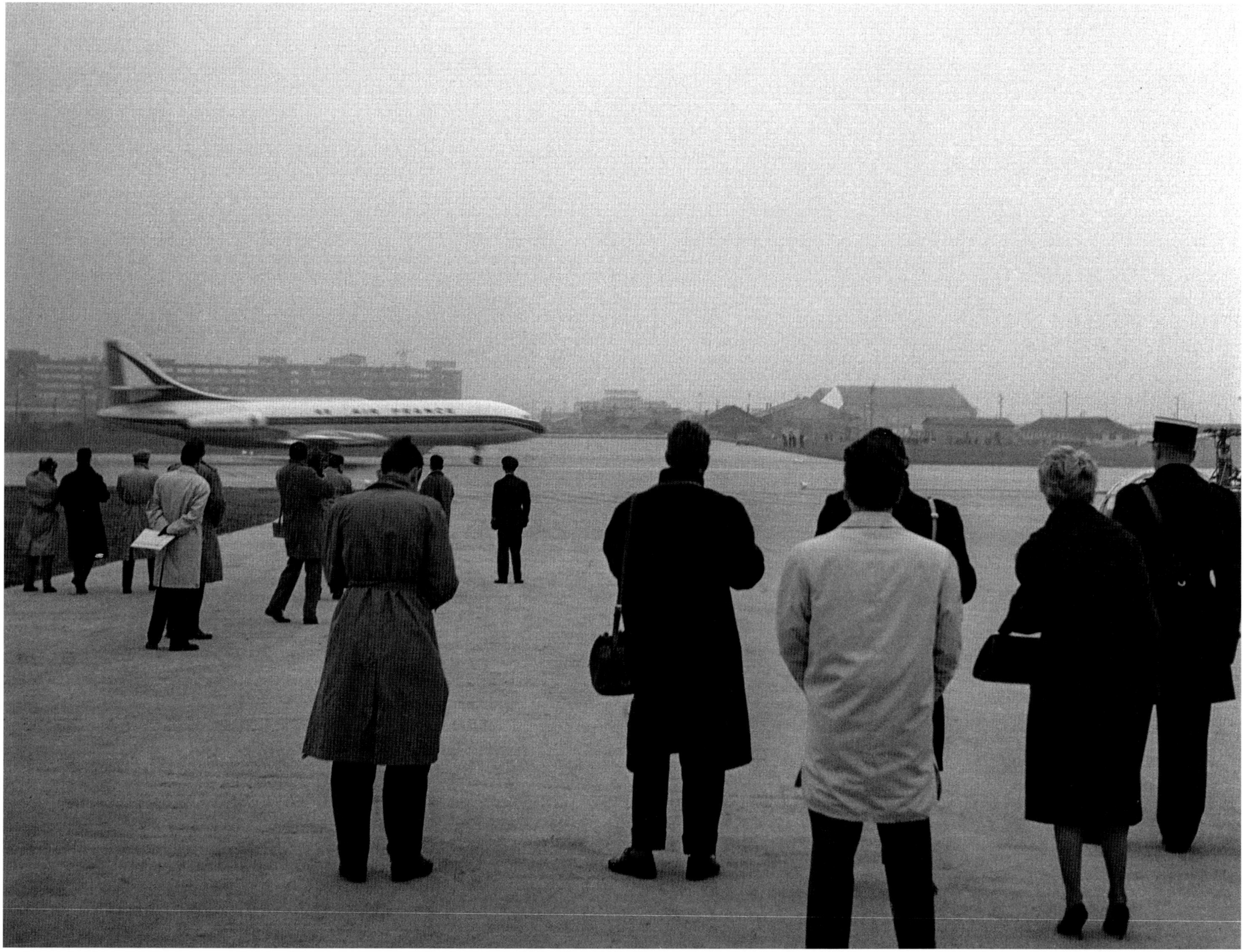

Opposite page: Opening of Runway 08-26 on 6 November 1959, in the presence of minister for public works and transport Robert Buron, Aéroport De Paris president Louis Couhé and Aéroport De Paris CEO Pierre Donatien Cot. In the background, a Caravelle.

Left: Gilbert Bécaud at Orly.

ORLYWOOD

They might be full-length features or short films, music videos, advertisements, or a fashion shoot. Airports are favorite settings for film directors. Every year, some forty shoots take place at Paris-Orly and Paris-Charles de Gaulle. Filming in these airports costs around 7,000 euros a day, and it's an important strand of public relations for Groupe ADP.

The history of the "seventh art" at Orly began in 1948 with Jean Delannoy's film *Aux yeux du souvenir*. In a chance meeting, an airhostess played by Michèle Morgan discovers that her former lover Jean Marais is captain of the plane. Nostalgia for the past and a narrowly avoided air accident serve to revive their love. In Jean-Luc Godard's 1960 *À bout de souffle*, Jean Seberg interviews writer Jean Parvulesco played by Jean-Pierre Melville, as he gets off the plane. In 1962, filmmaker Chris Marker made *La Jetée* at Orly, a famous short feature that was the inspiration for Terry Gilliam's *Twelve Monkeys*. A number of critics and filmmakers consider this experimental film to be a masterpiece.

Then in 1961, Orly Airport featured in Gilles Grangier's *Le cave se rebiffe*, with Jean Gabin; and featured again in 1964 in Philippe de Broca's *L'Homme de Rio* with Jean-Paul Belmondo. In 1967, Jacques Tati used Orly Airport as the basis for his imaginary town in *Playtime*. In Henri Verneuil's 1969 *Le Clan des Siciliens*, the clan led by Jean Gabin lays a trap for Alain Delon at the airport before being intercepted by the police. In 1972, Pierre Richard lands at Orly in Yves Robert's *Le Grand Blond avec une chaussure noire*, wearing one black and one yellow shoe. We also remember Yves Robert for the 1977 *Nous irons tous au paradis*, with the famous scene in the house at the end of the runway that was bought one day when the pilots were on strike. This huge property belonged for a long time to an Yves Robert fan who would gather once a month with his friends to re-enact the famous tennis match scene with the walls of the house shaking as airliners flew over. In 1973, Gérard Oury picked Orly for one of the most famous scenes in the *Aventures de Rabbi Jacob*, with Louis de Funès and Claude Giraud.

Many foreign directors have also brought their cameras to Orly. In 2002, Brian De Palma filmed *Femme fatale* here. Jacques Audiard and Luc Besson liked to use the terrace on the fourth floor at Orly South. The terrace has also served as backdrop for the triumphant arrival of celebrities such as France Gall in June 1966 returning from her tour of Japan, proudly displaying the medal she won as Japan's most popular singer. Orly has been the scene of departure for concerts and film promotions around the world. Fernandel in his time took the stage here, borrowing a cap from a runway agent.

Celebrities passing through Orly.

Opposite page: Top, Orson Welles; below, Jean Gabin. Film posters for *La Jetée*, made by Chris Marker in 1962, and *À Bout de Souffle*, made by Jean-Luc Godard in 1960.

Left: Jean Marais.

Below: Mireille Darc.

Entrance to the Publicis cinema
on the first floor of Hall 1,
Orly Airport South Terminal.

Unidentified passenger accompanied by a huge cat!

Ursula Andress, Jean-Paul Belmondo and Catherine Deneuve.

Audrey Hepburn.

72

Zizi Jeanmaire baptizes TWA's Boeing 747 *Star of Paris*, 13 April 1970.

MODERNIZATION AND EXPANSION

1961-2000

IN THE 1960S AND 1970S, ORLY'S SOUTH TERMINAL RANKED AS A SIGNIFICANT SHOP WINDOW FOR FRANCE.

An oval sign on the RN7 highway urged motorists to "Visit Orly". Orly South became immediately famous, like the Maison de la Radio that was built in Paris in the same period, and quickly became more than a simple travel facility. Bars, restaurants and especially the terraces quickly became visitor attractions. Gilbert Bécaud sang *Dimanche à Orly* and popularized the Parisian airport. The press at home and abroad made free use of superlatives as they praised the excellence of this location. "Orly, one of the most modern airports in the world," enthused *Libération*; "a marvel, the vestibule of France," declared *Le Figaro*. You went to Orly for its modernity, for the doors that opened all on their own, for the escalators, for the luxury of the space, with its light, its great windows, its marble floors, for its "Ding, ding, ding … now arriving from …," that smooth mythical voice that summoned up images of the world's most exotic locations. With more than three million visitors in 1963 and nearly four million two years later, the South Terminal became very quickly the most visited tourist site in France, ahead of the Eiffel Tower. People came to Orly South to dine at Les Trois Soleils, at the Tournebroche grill, or the Corbeille tea rooms.

"Sundays were incredibly busy, 1000 settings a day," remembers Christin, former chef at Les Trois Soleils, who joined as a trainee in 1965. People came to Orly to watch a film at the Publicis Orly cinema. Facilities included the 16-room Air Hotel for flight crews or passengers in transit.

While Orly drew visitors and excited popular curiosity, it was also concerned for the wellbeing of residents in neighboring communities. A *Bureau des Riverains* (service for local residents) was set up and participated in the promotion of the new site. Because quite apart from its tourist appeal, the expansion of the airport served to stimulate economic development in the locality. The international market was transferred to Rungis, which gave a considerable boost to the growth in airfreight business. At this time, Orly Airport handled nearly 100,000 tons of cargo per year. A Raymond Loewy designed Hilton Hotel opened on 25 October 1965, with 268 sound-proofed rooms.

Traffic grew exponentially. From six million passengers in 1965, the number of passengers handled by the South Terminal in 1969 had grown to nine million, half as much again as its planned capacity. The ten million passenger threshold was passed in 1971.

The South Terminal was in urgent need of enlargement. Working with three other architects, Henri Vicariot set about designing a second terminal. The construction of Orly West commenced in 1967.

The opening took place on 24 February 1971, after three years of work. This new terminal consisted of three halls devoted to domestic traffic, and was laid out in a pattern that was new for the times, with departures on the first floor and arrivals on the ground floor. It gave direct access to parking for more than 3,800 vehicles. The Orly South Terminal was later re-organized with a similar layout. Vicariot wanted to make the distance between car and plane as short as possible, and make it possible for passengers to join their plane as close as possible to the departure time. The concept he applied was simple, and channeled passengers to the planes in record time. Runway 4 was also now added, 3,650m long, to the north-west of the buildings. Runway 3 was extended to 3,320m with a brand new landing beacon system, reaching out to the south of the terminals and crossing the RN7 highway.

Now Orly Airport had two nearly parallel east-west runways. The first telescopic walkways came into service, attaching to the aircraft for the boarding and disembarking of passengers – no more coming and going by bus across the tarmac. Some of these walkways would have a reach of 47m. For the first time, tractors were introduced to shunt the planes backwards, a technique that would come to be used at the future Roissy-Charles de Gaulle Airport. Baggage was loaded in containers shaped to fit the holds of the aircraft, and delivered by conveyor belt. This was a real revolution that saved significant time for passengers.

It was also time to build a new control tower. Vicariot and his teams went back to work. The idea to build it on the roof of the South Terminal was quickly abandoned for practical reasons. The new tower would be sited 100m from the building. It would be slightly more than 50m tall, making the observation deck on the tenth floor high enough to give the controller sight of the start of the most distant runway, a view of any movement on the ground and sight of any circling planes. Henri Vicariot was once again inspired by what he had seen in the United States and proposed a tower with a twelve-sided dodecagonal shape. This would minimize the reflections inherent in the square observation decks that were common at the time, and give controllers the best possible view of all runways. The windows of the new tower were inclined at 15° to direct reflections towards the ceiling. They were treated on the inside with a thin coating of gold.

Special lighting was developed for the observation deck and the room where the radar screens were located. The air conditioning was carefully tuned to avoid all risk of misting on the windows.

Work on the control tower commenced in 1964 and was completed two years later with an inauguration of the new building along with Runway 4 by the then minister for public works Edgard Pisani. The runways were furnished with the very latest equipment: an ILS (Instrument Landing System) for landing in all weather, recorders, telecommunications and radar. The oil crisis being then a thing of the future, one of the main runways was fitted with a fog dispersal system, so aircraft could land in fog. A jet engine was installed at the end of the runway to raise the temperature by several degrees, which changed the air's moisture saturation capacity and thus dispelled the fog.

More modernization was yet to come, for the benefit of passengers and for the benefit of the airlines – a continuing stream of projects followed by the works that they entailed.

From the Boeing factories in Everett in Washington State came the 747, the plane that would democratize air travel. On 9 April 1970, the first of eight 747s ordered by Air France landed at Orly. Plans were urgently needed for departure and arrivals halls to accommodate this Jumbo Jet. The jet was put into service between Orly and New York, then Orly and Montreal, and eventually to the West Indies, Japan and the rest of the world. Hereafter the 747s would operate alongside 707s, Caravelles and the 737s. Traffic jams on the A6 freeway were becoming a problem. So in May 1972, SNCF introduced Orly Rail between Paris and Pont de Rungis, with buses to complete the link to the airport.

Two events marked 1974. The first was a new competitor for Boeing in the form of Airbus. On 15 April 1974, the first A300B landed at Orly and commenced service to London several weeks later. The second event was the opening of the new Roissy-Charles de Gaulle airport.

In light of predicted saturation at Orly, it had been decided in 1964 that a new airport had to be built, this time to the north of Paris. It opened on 1 April 1974, ten years after architect Paul Andreu started his drawings. Its first terminal, dubbed the Camembert, was a circular building served by a runway 3,600m long. From this moment, all attention seemed to point to the north of the capital. But Orly still had a case to make for itself.

The West Terminal has its admirers. It is much bigger than it looks and is well positioned between the runways, so the taxi-ing distance for planes is less. On a return journey to London or Zurich, the time a customer spends in the air and in the airport may be cut by nearly an hour compared to Orly South. Air France was just about convinced that this was the best place for all of its international and intra-European flights. But despite the numerous advantages of Orly West, it was forced to move to Roissy-Charles de Gaulle. The decision was largely political. One suspects that at the highest level of government opinion was that without the presence of Air France, the opening of Roissy-Charles de Gaulle would have failed. "The economy of Air France was sacrificed in the national interest," wrote former Air France director Jacques Bankir in his book *De Concorde aux low-cost*. Ultimately, it was the passengers of Lufthansa, Swissair and Alitalia who were first to profit from the new Orly West Terminal.

There was another company that would prosper thanks to Orly and its West Terminal – Air Inter. At the time, Air Inter was not yet a part of Air France, and it had had a difficult start in the 1960s. But now the company would profit from a monopoly in one very specific and ill-rewarded area, short-haul internal flights, a business that had lost foreign competitors a lot of money. As a private company Air Inter had proved highly vulnerable in its early years of existence. But with the State behind it, it now had the means to protect itself effectively by means of a series of agreements. Public powers guaranteed the company a *vocation privilégiée* (protected purpose) for internal airline business, a monopoly on the 18 most important routes in the network. The management strategy was simple: boost productivity by picking planes of the right size.

The bigger the plane, the lower the unit cost. In 1975, Air Inter ordered its first Airbus A300Bs. With more than 300 seats, they were double the size of its Mercures.

The business achieved growth of more than 11% per annum. The problem now was not attracting passengers, but finding them a seat.

Air Inter was a "low cost" flier ahead of its time. It developed a pricing system based on blue flights, white flights and red flights, a commercial innovation that would be copied by the car-hire companies. Within several years, with Orly as the base airport, nearly 60% of the population was just one hour by plane from Paris. Business travelers learned the benefit of there-and-back day trips. This company brought about a real democratization of air travel, and it dominated the Orly West Terminal. At its high point, the number of passengers carried by Air Inter passed the 17 million mark.

But clouds began to gather at the end of the 1980s, as Air Inter tried to win European routes to compensate for the serious impact of the TGV on the routes that had been most profitable. Having lost the battle for Marseille, Nice and Bordeaux, it picked up the crumbs of Air France medium-haul routes. In 1990, Air France bought UTA, which owned slightly more than 35% of Air Inter shares and, in this ricochet fashion, won control of the domestic carrier. From that point, there was trench warfare between Air Inter and its mother company.

Cycle track around the perimeter of Orly Airport in 1963.

Air Inter's Hangar N6 in the North Industrial Zone, March 1991.

The then director general of Air France Christian Blanc had just one obsession: to repatriate Air France's residual traffic from Orly South to Orly West, and above all to split the companies that were installed there. He being the savior of Air France, the State could not refuse him. And he was proved right. The private companies AOM, Corsair and Air Liberté were begged to transfer to Orly South. AOM president Marc Rochet was deaf to entreaties and had his planes painted with the message "We want to stay at Orly West." Since they did not occupy the entire terminal, Air France and Air Inter were ultimately joined by the Portugese carrier TAP, Spanish Iberia then later British Airways.

Other companies like Corsair, AOM, Minerve, and the Air France affiliate Air Charter International also played their part in the story of French airline successes. With the encouragement of Jacques Maillot, boss of travel agents Nouvelles Frontières, Corsair introduced the mass transport business of charter flights to France. The Caravelles of this little Corsican company, painted by hand in a hangar at Orly, were sold and replaced by Boeing 737s, then 747s. The aircraft were packed to accommodate 613 passengers, crew included. There had never been so many people on a plane. The liberalization of transport allowed Jacques Maillot to fly to the West Indies, Réunion, Dakar, Bangkok, Tahiti and Montreal. Sunny destinations were the big thing. In 1981, for the first time in the history of Orly Airport, the target of 100 passengers per plane was passed, and the number of occupied seats improved continuously. Car parks expanded. With more than 16,000 parking places, Orly Airport was at that time the biggest car park in France. In 1999 the Orlyval link was created, connecting the airport to the Antony RER station, using the VAL automatic transport system developed for the Lille metro and now also used in Rennes and Toulouse. Average journey time: 35 minutes. Road then joined up with rail with the addition of bus connections – Air France buses between the centre of Paris and the airport.

The South Terminal celebrated its thirtieth birthday in 1991, having handled somewhat more than 26 million passengers, compared with 16 million at Orly West. Orly was now France's premier airport. Several new projects were undertaken at Orly West, such as the new Hall 4 at the south end of the terminal.

So as not to waste the precious hours left vacant by the cancelling of Nantes, Toulon, Perpignan and Séville services, Air Inter in 1991 introduced a service called *La Navette* on its most profitable routes – a concept that would be spread elsewhere and picked up several years later by Air France on the Orly-Marseille and Orly-Toulouse routes, then extended to other towns. The idea was to offer a flight every 30 minutes to these destinations. The price war with Air Liberté had started and the passenger was the winner. But Air Liberté could not match the strength of the national carrier.

In 1994 a page of history turned when Air Inter disappeared forever and all of its activities were subsumed under the brand name Air France Europe, the final stage in a 35-year saga that had left a lasting mark on the French scene. Air Inter was defeated by competition from the train, and the intransigence of pilots who staged a long strike against the two-man piloting of the Airbus A320.

The same year, following a series of actions by residents in the area, the number of aircraft movements at Orly was limited to 250,000 per year, though the airport could handle up to 400,000.

The schedule slots, a priceless factor, were thereafter managed by Cohor, the association for the coordination of schedules, put in place by the transport minister. In June 1967, residents of communities bordering the airport, sick of the noise of planes, expressed their anger in a court action against Aéroports de Paris. A night-time ban from 23.30h to 06.00h was put in place in April 1968, by order of the minister.

For the airlines this was a hard blow and a serious operational constraint. Paradoxically, it was at this very moment that agreements were struck for the deregulation of air traffic – "clear skies," as it was known – first in the United States, then in Europe, and new carriers were appearing accordingly. The residents did not back down and, in the face of this pressure, the government put certain measures in place. Lines of approach and departure were modified and help was offered to residents close to the airport to improve the sound-proofing of their homes. Several homes in the noisy zone were bought up and demolished.

But the curfew imposed by residents to limit the nuisance did discourage certain airlines. One after another, they moved to Roissy-Charles de Gaulle. The prestige of the southern Paris airport decreased. Roissy-Charles de Gaulle grew, stole the limelight and captured all the investment. The petrol crisis of 1973 had already struck a blow against the site. With the disappearance of the most fuel-greedy planes like the 707-120, Orly had given up a large part of its transatlantic traffic to specialize in flights to Africa and the Near and Middle East. At the end of the 1990s, traffic diminished and the attraction of Orly was broken. The South airport was under-used. Traffic reduced by stages from 27 million passengers in 1996 to 22.5 million in 2003. Orly is all the same well regarded as much by clients as by airlines for its central location and its flexibility. For several years, it has attracted new interest, and this has proved a key factor in the development of Greater Paris. —

ORLY WAS ONE OF THE SYMBOLS OF FRANCE'S REVIVAL IN THE 1960S, ALONGSIDE NUCLEAR ENERGY, THE CARAVELLE, THE *FUSÉE DIAMANT* SATELLITE LAUNCH ROCKET, THE LINER *FRANCE*, MYSTÈRE FIGHTERS AND CONCORDE. THE MAGNIFICENT AIR TERMINAL DESIGNED BY HENRI VICARIOT AND OPENED BY GENERAL DE GAULLE IN 1961 ENJOYS A RIGHTFUL PLACE ON THIS EXTRAORDINARY LIST.

Patrick Gandil, CEO of the Directorate General for Civil Aviation

Opposite page: Baggage hall, October 1961.

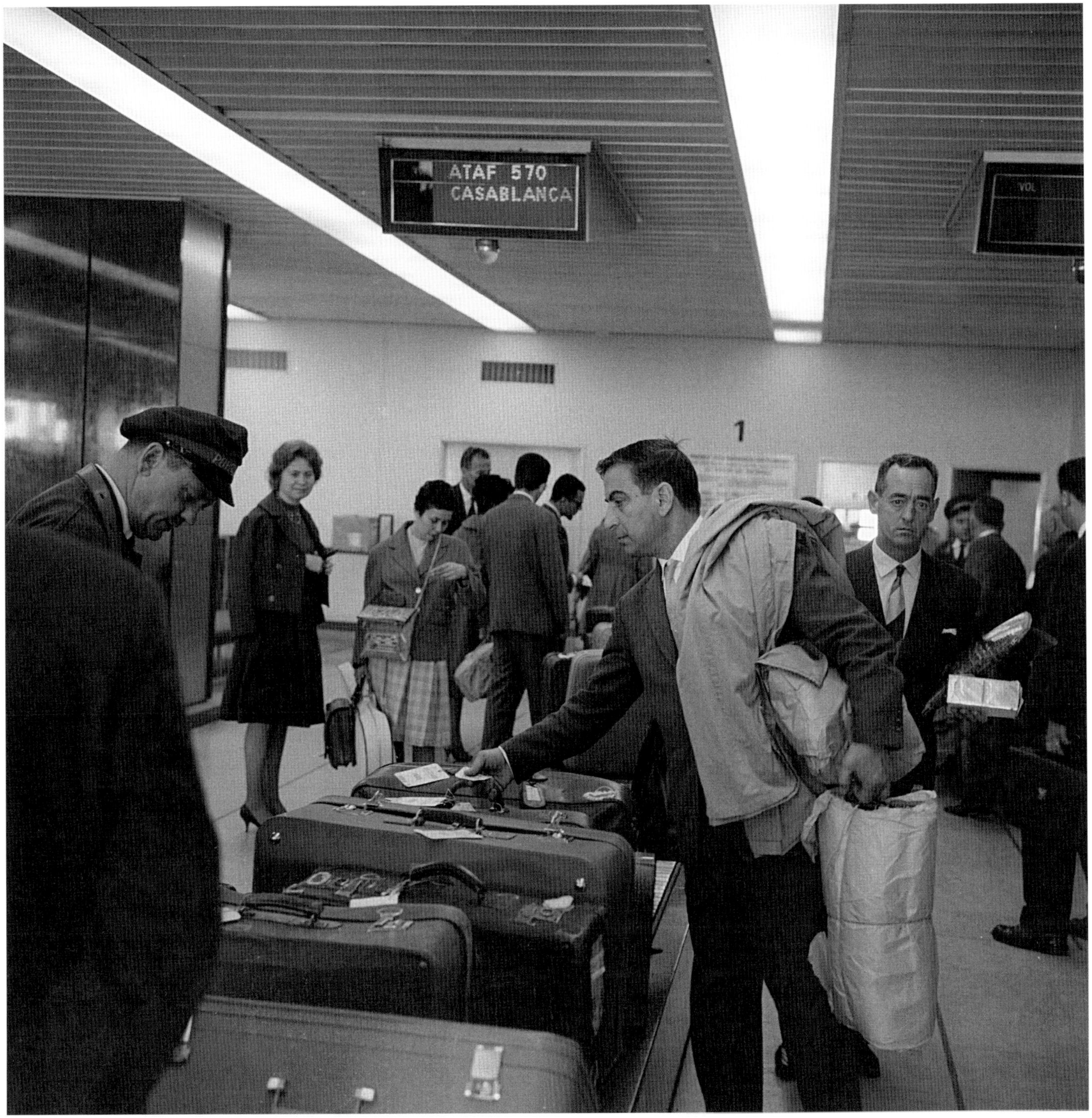
ATAF 570
CASABLANCA
VOL
1

The Trois Soleils restaurant, with wall hanging by Jean Lurçat, June 1961.

The "Voice of Orly" – the hostess who made the terminal announcements at the microphone, October 1961.

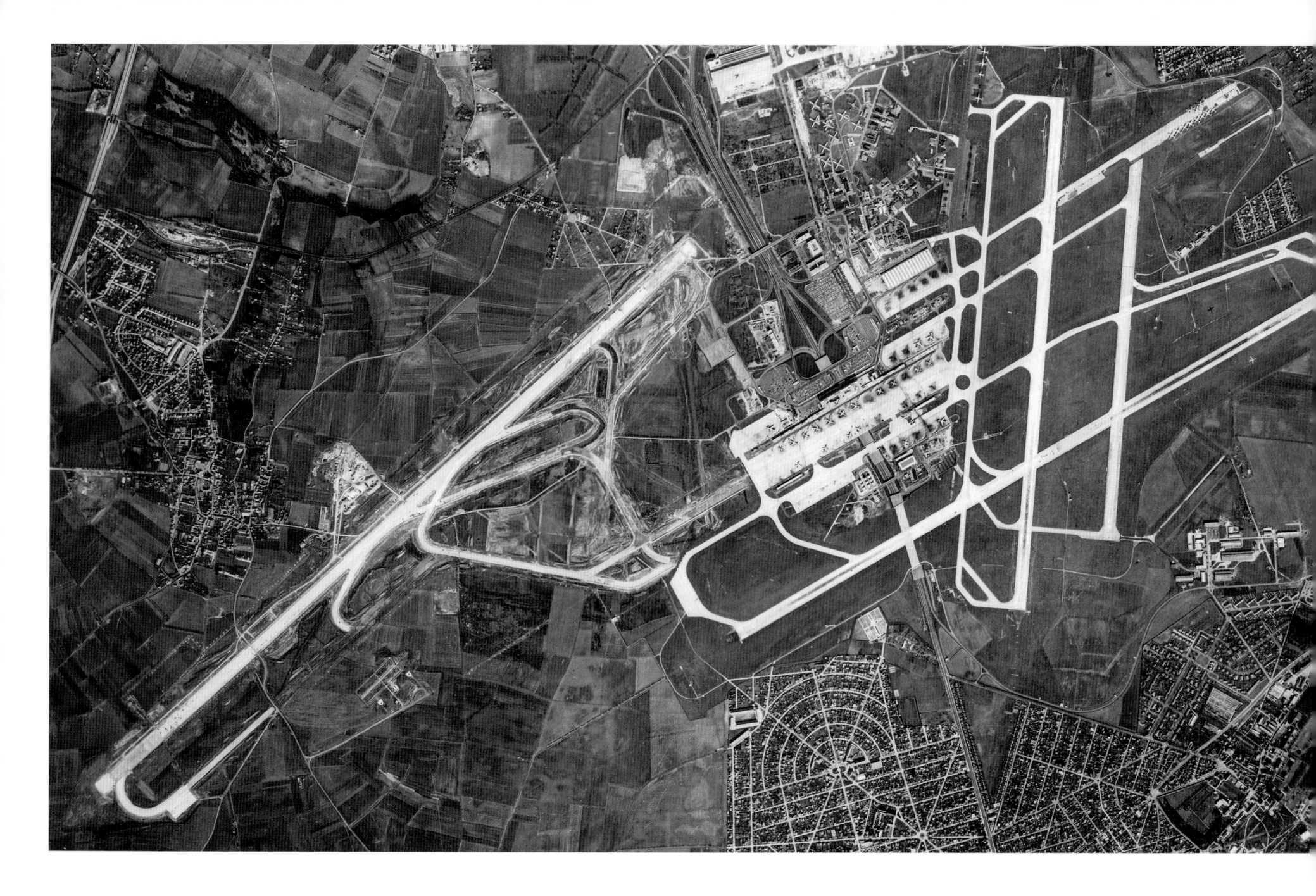

Aerial view of Orly in 1965.

Visitors on the terraces watching a Caravelle, March 1966.

Full-scale trials of the
first telescopic walkways,
12 June 1968.

Jet-engine fog clearing system installed at the south end of Runway 4, October 1970.

The West and South Terminals in July 1970.

CONCORDE

Nearly all of the aircraft that have revolutionized the history of modern air flight have passed through Orly Airport. Just one is missing: Concorde. Appearances of the supersonic have been fairly rare, other than for purposes of certification before its introduction to commercial service in 1976. The product of close collaboration between Sud Aviation and the British Aircraft Corporation, Prototype 001 of this Franco-British supersonic craft had its first flight from Toulouse Blagnac on 2 March 1969 with a crew comprising test pilot and captain André Turcat, co-pilot Jacques Guignard, engineer Henri Perrier and mechanic Michel Rétif. The British prototype 002 followed on 9 April 1969 with Brian Trubshaw at the controls.

On 29 May, Concorde 001 flew over Paris at low altitude before joining the Bourget Air Show where it was the great star of the show. The revolutionary Boeing 747 Jumbo Jet flying in from the United States seemed a pale figure by comparison. On 1 October the same year, Concorde broke the sound barrier, then passed Mach 2 (2,000kph). Once the first test flights were complete, it made an extended tour of the whole world. Concorde flew to the United States after a stop-off in Las Palmas for the inauguration of the new airport at Dallas Fort Worth in Texas. On 26 September 1973, the supersonic craft completed a historic flight between Washington and Paris – the first direct flight across the North Atlantic by supersonic craft registration FWTSA, completed in three hours and 33 minutes. This would be one of its rare appearances at Orly.

The same day, Concorde left Orly for Toulouse for necessary maintenance. It was then 21 January 1976 before Air France operated its first commercial flights between Roissy-Charles de Gaulle and Rio via Dakar, the plane being banned from flying to New York because it was judged too noisy. Together with a huge hostile campaign in the United States and problems of commercialization, Concorde took a beating from the 1973 petrol crisis.

Finally in November 1977, after months of negotiation, the American authorities allowed Concorde into JFK Airport in New York. But it was too late. Despite its qualities, only 16 examples of this supersonic jewel of 1960s technology were ever produced, and sold to just two operators, Air France and British Airways. The prototype Concorde FWTSA ended its career in a parking space at Orly on 20 May 1976, along with the prototype Caravelle 01, another mythical craft. It was disarmed, the motors removed and certain parts salvaged. Once exhibited, the plane was more or less abandoned before it was bought for one franc by the town of Athis Mons. On the initiative of Nicolas Roland Payen, the inventor of the Delta wing, it was thereafter exhibited and open to visitors at the Delta museum, to the south of the airport by the side of the RN7 highway.

Air France Concorde passing through Orly on 1 September 1977.

Above: Building the Hilton Hotel in 1965.

Opposite page: Entrance to the car park in front of the West Terminal, when it opened in 1971.

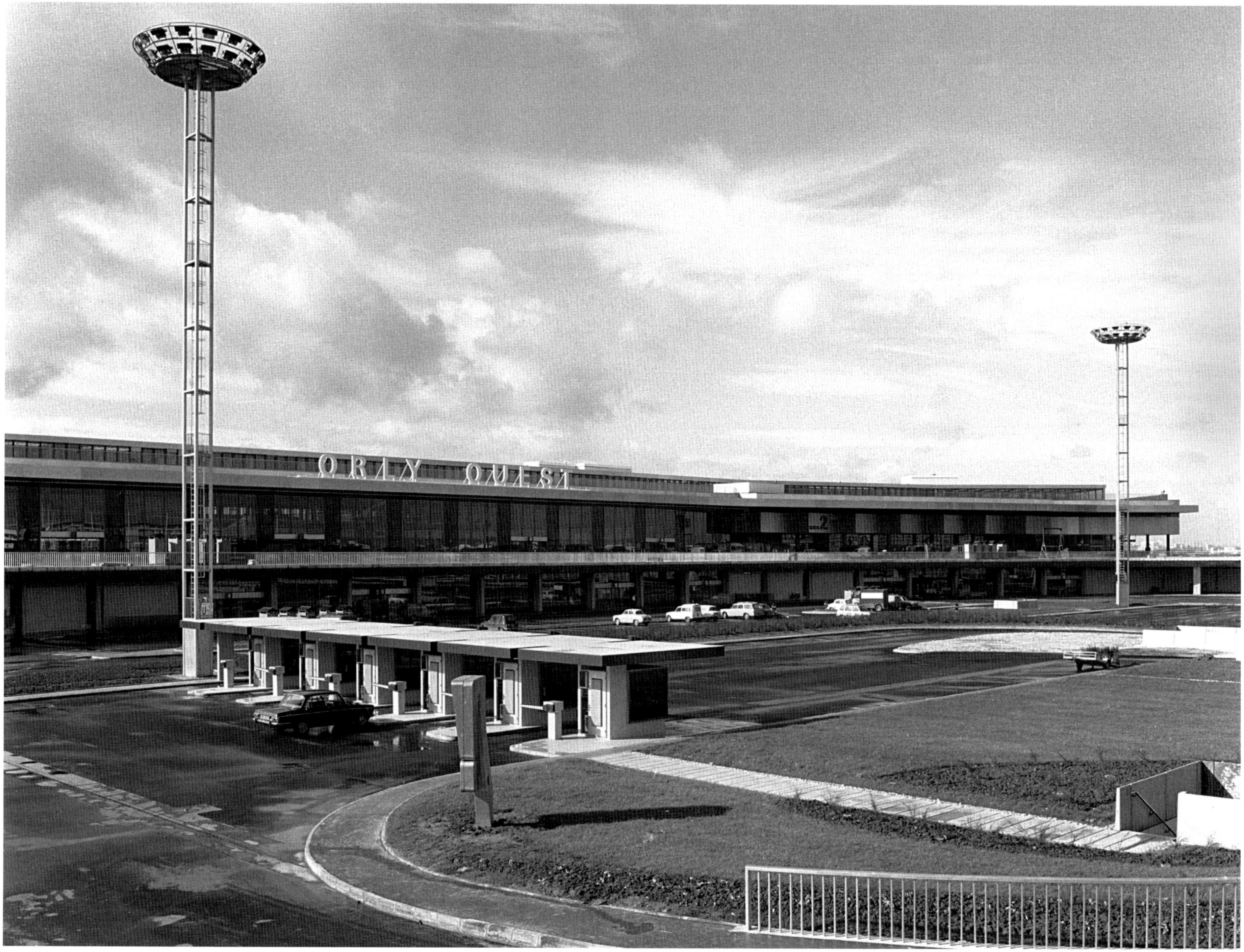
ORLY OUEST

SUNDAYS AT ORLY

In the 1960s, the France of General de Gaulle would crowd onto the Orly terraces to watch stars like Ursula Andress, Jean-Paul Belmondo or Brigitte Bardot be photographed as they left the plane. Perched on top of that "steel and glass giant", the terraces in those days received more than four million visitors each year. A lot more than the Eiffel Tower or the Palace of Versailles! Here parading stars shared the company of ordinary folk dressed in their Sunday best. "I was barely ten years old, and my father was impressed by these planes," remembers Charlotte who lives in Athis Mons. "He knew that this was the future, and we would come from Rouen to admire the scene." "At the time, Aéroports de Paris encouraged the simply curious to visit," says Lucio Pernotto, a painter of air scenes who has painted many pictures of Orly. "You could take an open-topped bus for a guided tour. Aéroports de Paris wanted flying to become a mode of mass transport."

Then came the end of Sundays at Orly, and the end of an era. In 1975, an attack launched from the terraces by the terrorist Carlos and three accomplices forced their closure for reasons of security. They had attempted to fire a rocket launcher at an El Al Boeing 747 as it took off. The attackers were spotted, guns were fired and 20 people were wounded, many seriously. Then the terraces were completely closed after the 1999 storm.

The Paris-Orly terrace re-opened in 2004, fitted with bullet-proof windows and safety nets. The terrace is located at the fourth and final level of the South Terminal: an area of 1,900m², of which 770m² is lawn with tables and chairs. The view over the tarmac and runways is unbeatable. Now once again you can relax in a seat and watch the take-off and landing of the planes. The terrace today is equipped with telescopes. This is certainly a long way from the thousands of tourists of the 1960s, but the dance of the planes still has its admirers – time for a coffee break, a telephone call or a quick picnic in a special place.

The Orly terraces in the 1960s.

The terraces of the first South Terminal in the 1950s.

The terraces of the new South Terminal in the 1960s.

"Rush hour" on the Orly terraces – a place to go for family outings.

A group of Native Americans arriving in 1966.

Above: Loading a TWA Boeing 747, February 1970.

Right: Local residents come to Orly to watch the first flight of the Airbus A300B, 18 January 1973.

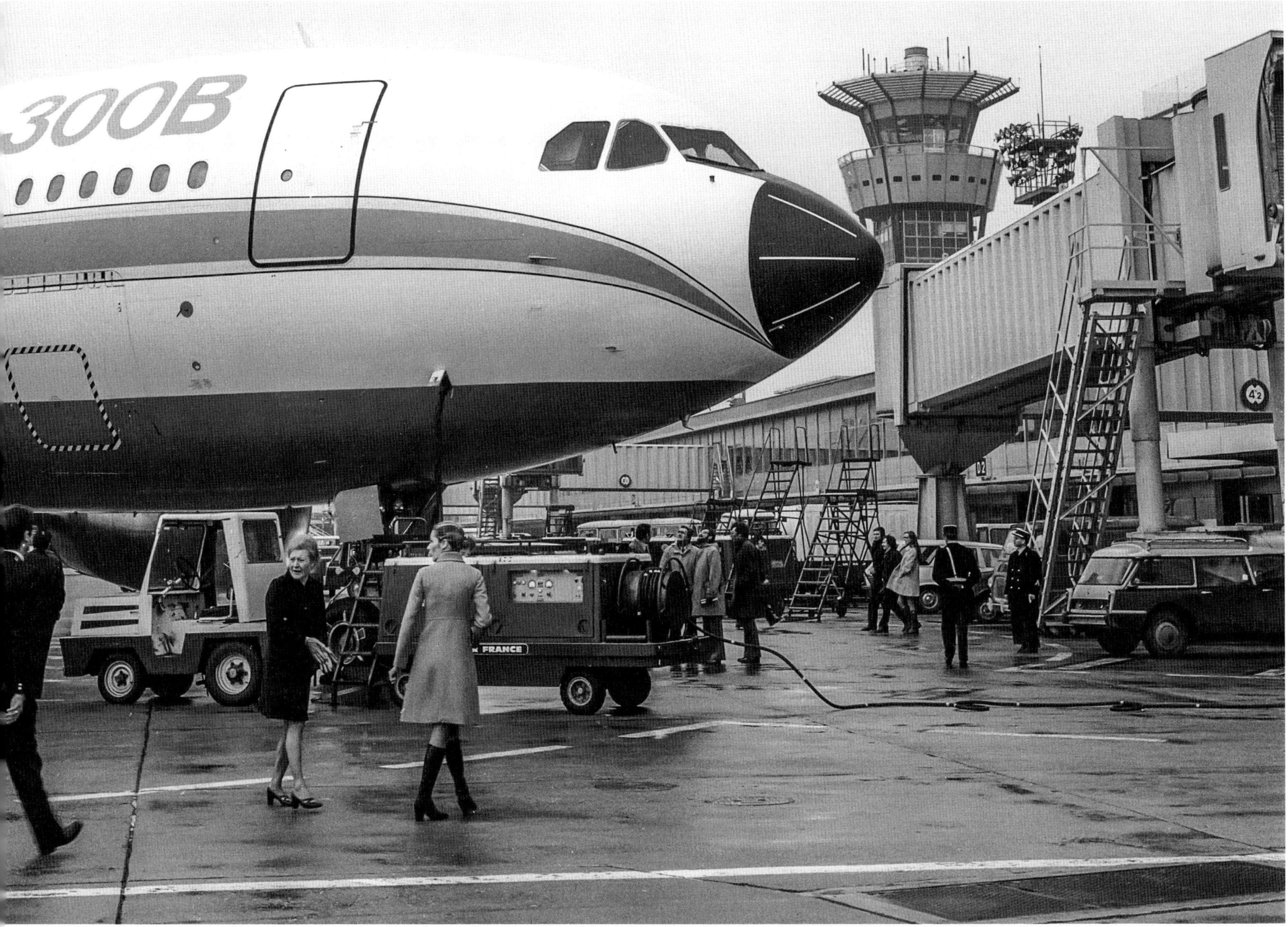
300B
FRANCE
D2
42

Telescopic walkway connects with Air Inter Airbus, May 1990.

Hall 1 of the West Terminal, September 1996.

ASTROLABE

Making the "Astrolabe, or movement of the Earth and Moon", installed in Orly's West Terminal in 1970.

The Astrolabe clock was conceived by architect Pierre Kayser and installed in 1970 to mark the opening of the West Terminal. It was restored in 1999. The clock is suspended from the ceiling of the terminal at the departures level on the first floor in the public area, and is the focal attraction of the entrance hall. A most useful instrument for any traveller who seeks information.

The astrolabe is an astronomic clock that represents the solar system. It shows the correct time for any place on Earth, the average sidereal time (the time in relation to the stars as opposed to the Sun), the time of sunrise and sunset, the average longitude of the Moon, the phases of the Moon and the Sun in relation to the signs of the Zodiac, the eclipses of the Sun and the Moon and the ascending node. The clock advances by four minutes every day by comparison with a classic clock.

Its sophisticated mechanisms were crafted by the Strasbourg company Ungerer, in the person of engineer Henri Bach. They display Earth-Moon rotation and the movements of the pair around the Sun (fixed), as also the celestial movements across a 24-hour period at a scale of 1:7,000,000. The clock weighs nearly five tons and measures 6.34m wide by 4m high. It is one of the emblems of the Paris-Orly West Terminal.

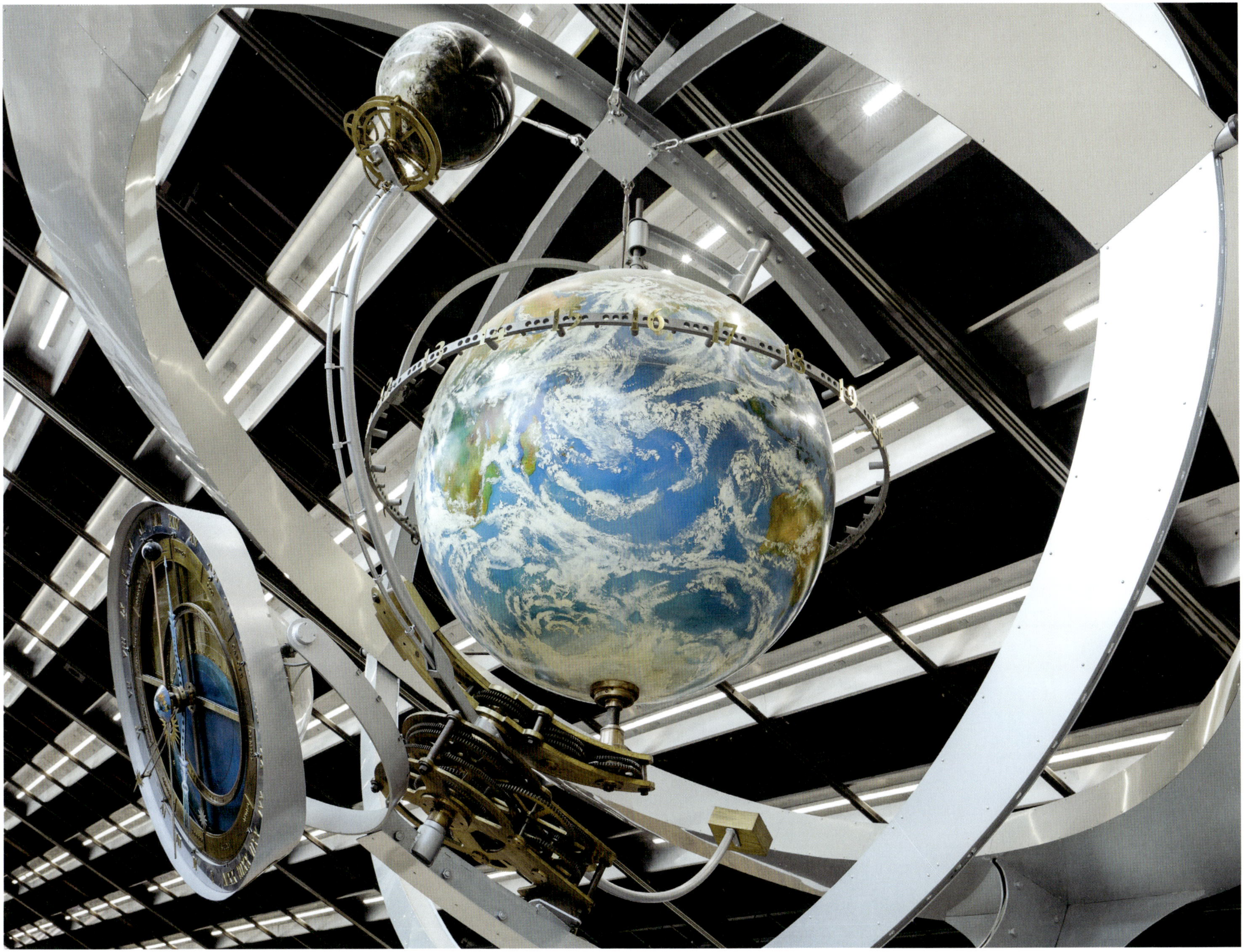
16
17
18

THE AIRPORT
IN THE CITY

PARIS-ORLY TODAY

IT IS FIVE O'CLOCK AND ORLY IS WAKING UP. THE SHOPS IN THE TWO TERMINALS ARE RAISING THEIR SHUTTERS.

The first departing passengers have already passed through the checkpoints. The first flight takes off at six. Businessmen and tourists are drinking a peaceful coffee, reading the day's newspaper and checking emails. Offstage the shadowy workforce that's hidden from public view is busy. The performance on the ground and in the air begins.

The players include air traffic controllers, ramp agents, refuellers, machine operators, baggage handlers, maintenance staff, flight preparation staff, station staff, reception staff, customs officers, firemen and cooks. The list could be much longer. Today nearly 27,000 people work day and night on the Paris-Orly site – the essential cogs in this well-oiled airport machine where everything is timed, planned and perfectly co-ordinated.

It's "action stations" for the airlines' station agents to check in and board passengers without wasting any time. No more than two minutes is the average per passenger. Speed is of the essence, avoiding queues at the check-in desks. In the duty manager's office, it is time for the morning briefing. Around the table are gathered the human resources managers, operations managers and Groupe ADP facilities managers, and the station managers. First matter of the day: "How many flights are out there today? Ah yes, the Rome flight, it should be in contact." "OK, can we re-schedule the Spanish 747? It is not leaving until tomorrow." The phones ring continuously. Six o'clock.

Meanwhile on the runway, a ground handling agent picks up his jacket and orange vest and hurries to Alfa 5, the space where a flight from Toulouse is expected to park, ready to guide the aircraft on the ground and supervise the sequence of operations. Once the aircraft has landed, it's a race against the clock. The plane approaches, following signals given by the aircraft marshaller, turns gently and stops. From up in his cockpit, the captain gives a thumbs-up signal. The motors are cut and the walkway is attached. The baggage-handling teams open the hold. The re-fuelling truck is already in place. A hose is connected between the plane's fuel tank and the supply point on the ground. A note on the cockpit window says 9.5 tons. That's the quantity of fuel required for the next flight. The baggage has meanwhile left the plane. The tank is filled, the plane is cleaned.

And already it's time to leave again. The passengers start to board. The ground handling agent talks to the crew. The walkway is withdrawn. The "pusher" tractor that reverses the plane now comes into play. A metal bar is attached to the landing gear, and the driver lines up the aircraft on the taxiway.

Another hand sign. "Have a good flight, have a good journey," signals the ground handling agent. All is OK. "Orly Sol on 121.705, we are ready to depart," calls the co-pilot. Life here follows the rhythm of the planes.

The over-riding objective is to anticipate and so far as possible minimize the turn-round time. The smallest delay has financial consequences for everyone in the chain, including sub-contractors. The "low cost" revolution is driven by this principle.

Airside and landside, the Gendarmerie des Transports Aériens (GTA) is working on all fronts. They supervise the security of the airport, checking identities, watching over people, baggage, suspect packages, dealings of any kind, incidents and accidents.

Before the first take-offs and landings, the day begins with an inspection of the runways by Groupe ADP agents. They must be sure there's no foreign object on the tarmac that might be a danger to flights. This process will be repeated three or four times in the day, like the inspection of the thirty kilometers of taxiways down which the aircraft move to reach their stopping points. Birds are also a risk to planes. At dawn, the bird-scarers begin their patrol. There's a dozen men in vehicles at Orly ready to scare off any bird that might strike an aircraft and cause serious damage. Gas cannons, bird distress calls, noise makers – all available methods are used to chase off the birds. These are the men of the avian risk prevention team, a structure established in July 1989 at all nationally important airports.

Trimming vegetation on the borders of the runways also plays an important role in managing avian risks, and maintenance here is crucial for the security of flights. If a plane goes off the runway, the grass serves as a shock-absorbing carpet. But if the grass is too long, the grass stalks oscillate and may create a frequency that interferes with radio communications. These areas are serviced by Groupe ADP agents at night when no further commercial flights are expected. Time too to check the runway lights that guide the pilots on approach, a precious aid to aircraft navigation. More than 10,000 lights are inspected every day and replaced as necessary.

At the other end of the runways, in Air France Industries' huge hangars, mechanics and engineers fuss over the planes that will be taking off in the coming hours. Others may remain for several days for more in-depth maintenance. Paris-Orly is also the place where, day and night, they prepare the thousands of meals that are served on the planes. Top-flight gastronomy for business class and first class, more simple for economy class, but all are prepared with the same concern for quality and hygiene. No risks are taken. The consequences of food poisoning among passengers or crew on a plane would be catastrophic. At Paris-Orly, Gategroup subsidiary Servair employs nearly 300 staff to make the dishes that will be served on the planes.

The airport has a life of its own that never stops. It is a town within the town, a micro-society where everybody knows everybody else. Despite the scale of its passenger numbers – 31 million in 2016, equivalent to half the French population – Paris-Orly has managed to retain a human dimension, almost like a family. Franck Mereyde, director of the airport from 2011 to 2017, says: "Paris-Orly is part of the heart of the town and its evolutions, preparing itself to become an airport inside the boundaries of Paris. That is part of what gives it its futuristic character."

Paris-Orly is today the Number Two French airport after Paris-Charles de Gaulle. Just 12km from Paris, its area today is more than 1,600 hectares, the same as a town like Nancy. Its boundaries extend across several communes – Orly, Villeneuve le Roi, Paray Vieille Poste, Wissous, Athis Mons and Chilly Mazarin. The airport is an integrated part of an important economic hub within the Île de France which includes most notably the Marché d'Intérêt National (MIN, the Rungis International Market) with its road haulage centre, business parks, buildings and offices operated by the SILIC; and the Belle Épine commercial centre.

Today the airport has three runways, two running parallel east-west to suit prevailing winds for landing and take-off, and a third north-south which is rarely used. At peak times, an aircraft takes off and lands every 50 seconds. Plane movements may be restricted to 250,000 per year, but the number of passengers is on the increase by on average around 3-4% per annum. Why? Because the airlines are using the space in their aircraft more efficiently and the rate of seat occupation is always improving. In parallel with this growth, the number of flights is reducing. So in 2017, we are a long way from the limit set in 1994.

Once again today, Paris-Orly holds a special place in the hearts of the French. Its history has earned it a terrific level of affection. Having been abandoned at the beginning of the 1990s, Orly then won renewed interest from airlines and travelers alike. It owes this attachment to a number of natural advantages, starting with its closeness to the capital. The airport is entirely located inside the perimeter of Greater Paris. Another advantage for the airlines is the short taxi time. It takes on average just six minutes for an airplane to get from the terminal to the point of take-off. As says EasyJet's French director François Bachetta: "This is a considerable advantage and an essential factor in the development of low-cost carriers operating on short- and medium-distance routes with point-to-point flights."

The economic model is built on very short turn-round times, no more than 35-40 minutes. That's why Orly has become the preferred airport for companies like EasyJet, Vueling or the Air France subsidiary Hop.

In the course of recent years, connections to Europe have multiplied, with nearly 70 towns in Europe now served. What's more, the market for low-cost services is expanding, including busy businessmen attracted by the reduced journey time of services like the Air France shuttle that offers there-and-back excursions in a single day. The traffic of low-cost carriers at Paris-Orly today represents a little more that a third of the 234,450 movements counted on the site in 2016. By way of example, EasyJet accounted for some forty flights a day. In total, 32 operators land and take off at Orly. Together they serve 41 countries and 150 destinations.

The West Terminal accommodates a large proportion of the short-haul flights of Air France and its subsidiary Hop with the Navette. Air France operates the premier European domestic network. Alongside at the West Terminal are a number of low-cost operators such as EasyJet, Vueling, Air Europa and several international flights to New York, one operated by Air France, the others by British Airways subsidiary Open Skies. Hall A at the South Terminal is dedicated to international flights to North Africa, to the Near and Middle East and long-haul flights to the West Indies and the Indian Ocean. Hall B serves flights to Schengen destinations by Transavia, the low-cost operator of the Air France-KLM group with regular flights and charters to European destinations in and around the Mediterranean basin.

The new international pier at the South Terminal, opened in April 2016, today receives nearly 80% of passengers travelling outside the Schengen zone. Capacity is 1.9 million passengers per year. The building is particularly well lit, with large glazed bays looking out over the tarmac, faithful to the spirit established by Henri Vicariot in the 1960s. The floor is marble and the 950 seats in the waiting area all have power sockets. The pier is 180m long with an area of 12,000m^2 on two floors, one for boarding, one for disembarking. It is used most notably by Air Caraïbes, French Blue, Corsair, Transavia, Tunisair, Air Algérie and Aigle Azur. It can handle six jumbo-size planes or twelve medium-size planes and raises the proportion of gate parking positions to 90%. "This is an installation of the same quality, following the same architectural standards as Hall M of Terminal 2E at Paris-Charles de Gaulle," points out Groupe ADP president Augustin de Romanet. Groupe ADP has invested nearly 90 million euros in this building. The international pier is part of the modernization plan for Paris-Orly, which in the course of recent years has seen several large building projects set in motion, such as the refurbishing of the esplanades and entrances of the South and West Terminals and – looking forward to 2020 – the opening of the link between the two buildings. —

The runways at sunset.

Orly under curfew. No plane is allowed to take off or land at the south Paris airport between eleven thirty in the evening and six o'clock in the morning.

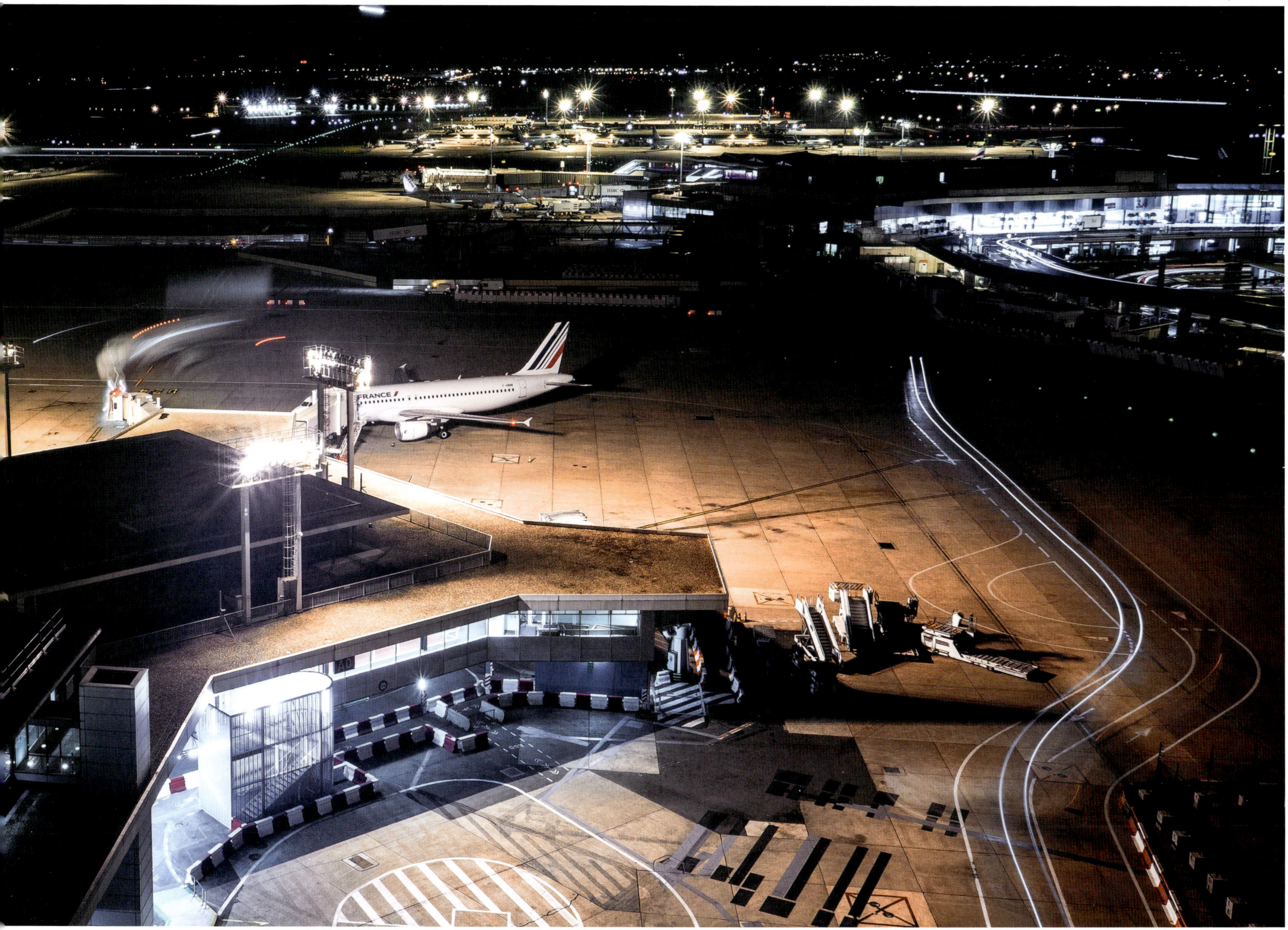
FRANCE

LANDING AND TAKE-OFF SLOTS

Below: Transavia Boeing 737-800 taking off.

Opposite page: The day begins at Paris-Orly.

Like most busy or very busy airports, Paris-Orly is classed as a Co-ordinated Airport. Every landing or take-off of an airline plane must happen in an agreed time slot. By statute dated 9 August 1996, the co-ordination of time slots is managed by the Association Pour la Coordination des Horaires, or Cohor. This independent association serves the main companies and airports of Paris, Nice and Lyon, with a co-ordinator for each country in Europe. Like Frankfurt and Geneva, Paris-Orly is subject to a daily curfew from 23.30h to 06.00h. No aircraft can land or take off in this period without a special dispensation, on pain of heavy fines. Paris-Orly is moreover limited to 250,000 time slots per year, of which 28,000 are reserved for flights *d'aménagement du territoire* (survey flights) and public service flights in general.

Time slots are a precious commodity that must be fairly allocated. A balance must be struck between the demands of airlines already in place and those that are new to the airport. A consultative committee operates under the presidency of the Direction Générale de l'Aviation Civile (DGAC). IATA (the International Air Transport Association) holds a conference for the coordination of time slots twice a year, in November for the following summer season and in June for the following winter season. It is open to coordinators and all airlines, whether or not they are members of IATA.

The allocation of time slots runs according to certain priorities. The first to be assigned are historic time slots (those that have been used by an airline for at least 80% of the period for which they have been allocated, if the airline still requires them). These slots can be shifted to a different time relative to the preceding equivalent season. We speak of this rule as "Right of the grandfather", or "Use it or lose it". At Paris-Orly as at Paris-Charles de Gaulle, Air France takes advantage of this rule to retain nearly 50% of its historic slots. To help new carriers get access to the market, the next priority goes to carriers who have less than 5% of slots at the airport, and operate routes between EU countries that are served by no more than three airlines. What's left is a pool of slots that are newly created, unused or abandoned and therefore available. Half of these slots are allocated to newcomers.

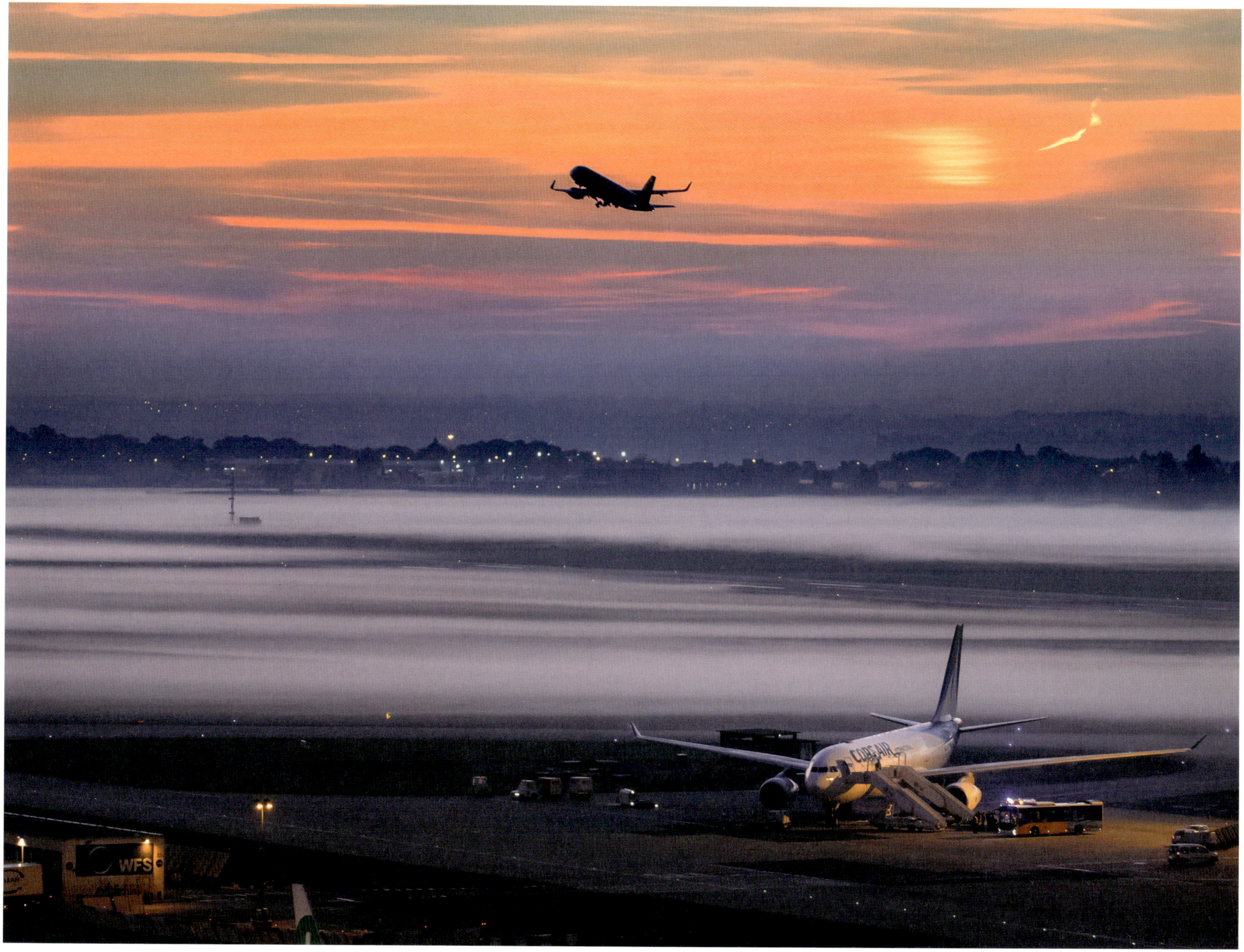
CORSAIR
WFS

Air France offers long-haul flights to the French West Indies from Paris-Orly, and a route to New York.

The Red Hippo in the West Terminal public area.

THERE'S A CURIOUS CONTRAST AT PARIS-ORLY, BETWEEN THE CALM OF THE NIGHT WHEN MAINTENANCE TAKES PLACE, AND THE TUMULTUOUS HOURS WHEN TRAVELLERS ARE ARRIVING AND LEAVING, FOR DESTINATIONS NEAR AND FAR.

Nathalie Stubler, director Transavia France

Opposite page: Waving goodbye to a flight for Istanbul.

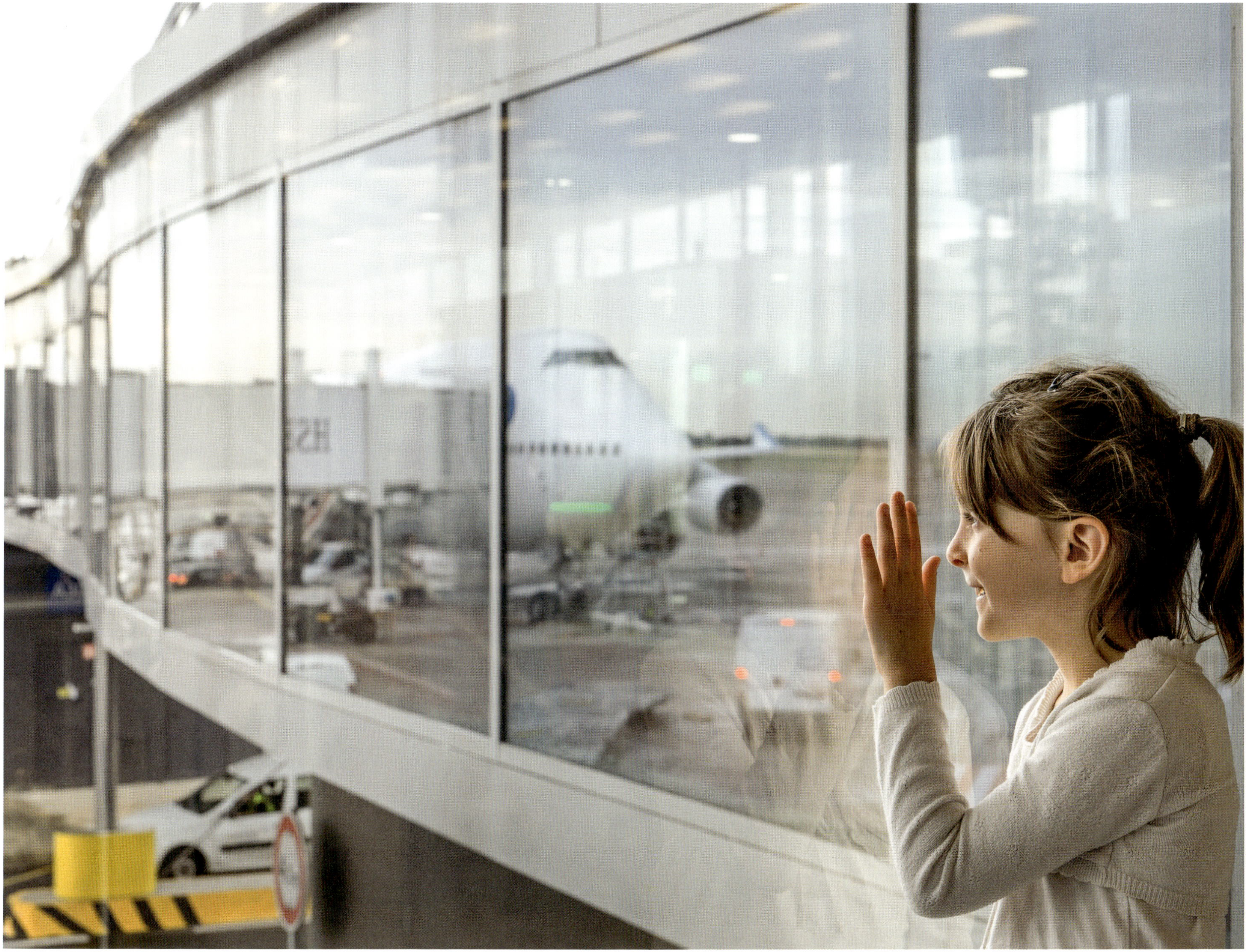

Taken from the exhibition *Regards en coulisses* (Looking behind the scenes).

Samilla, Securitas.

Leslie, MAC.

Denis, Le Marché Parisien.

Lydie, Orlyval.

SECURITY AND ATTENTION

The first terrorist attack on a French airport happened in the mid 1970s: a failed rocket attack against an El Al plane at Orly, by the Palestinian "Black November" group. The attacks of 11 September 2001 in the United States marked a change in awareness, and it was thereafter a priority to make airports as proof as possible against attack. But risk can never be reduced to zero. In March 2017, the attack on an Operation Sentinelle patrol at Paris-Orly reopened the debate on this complex issue and its limitations in areas open to the public. Some airports – though not Paris-Charles de Gaulle or Paris-Orly – have chosen to search passengers and baggage at the entrance to terminals, but this solution is controversial. The installations required are costly and ineffective, creating queues and concentrations of people who might then be the target for a terrorist attack.

In France, airport security costs around a billion euros per year, with a direct impact on the price of tickets. Nearly 5,000 personnel are dedicated to the surveillance of Groupe ADP's three main sites, at Paris-Charles de Gaulle, Paris-Orly and Le Bourget. These are the police, gendarmes, security agents, Groupe ADP personnel, dog teams and military teams of Operation Sentinelle. Police and information services lend support in public areas ahead of the baggage checking point. Air-side, the security role is handled by the Air Traffic Gendarmerie.

What's needed is a solution that does not interfere with the smooth movement of passengers and the constraints of landing and take-off time slots. With the constant increase in traffic, this is a formidable challenge for Groupe ADP. Much is invested to improve efficiency, like the reinforcement of the Parafe system for the automatic checking of passports, and the installation of 87 new airlocks between now and the spring of 2018. For some time, as in Israel and the United States, Paris-Charles de Gaulle and Paris-Orly have employed "profilers" mingling with the crowd and trained to spot suspect behavior. Nearly 9,000 cameras survey the two airports, from the parking to the boarding points. The next step when the law allows it would be a systematic link between surveillance cameras and the files of persons who are dangerous or suspect. Cameras with algorithms that detect suspect behavior already exist on the market. Meanwhile a system of face recognition is presently on trial at Paris-Charles de Gaulle. Eventually the aim would be to put in place a multitude of independent checks that would work together as a coherent system to complicate the task of possible terrorists.

It is the job of security personnel to check passengers, and scan cabin baggage and personal effects.

The bangs of rockets, sudden alarm sounds, laser beams, imitations of bird distress calls – everything is used to chase away the birds.
The battle against avian risk is one of the jobs for Groupe ADP agents.

The new Groupe ADP fire station, with crews on stand-by around the clock.

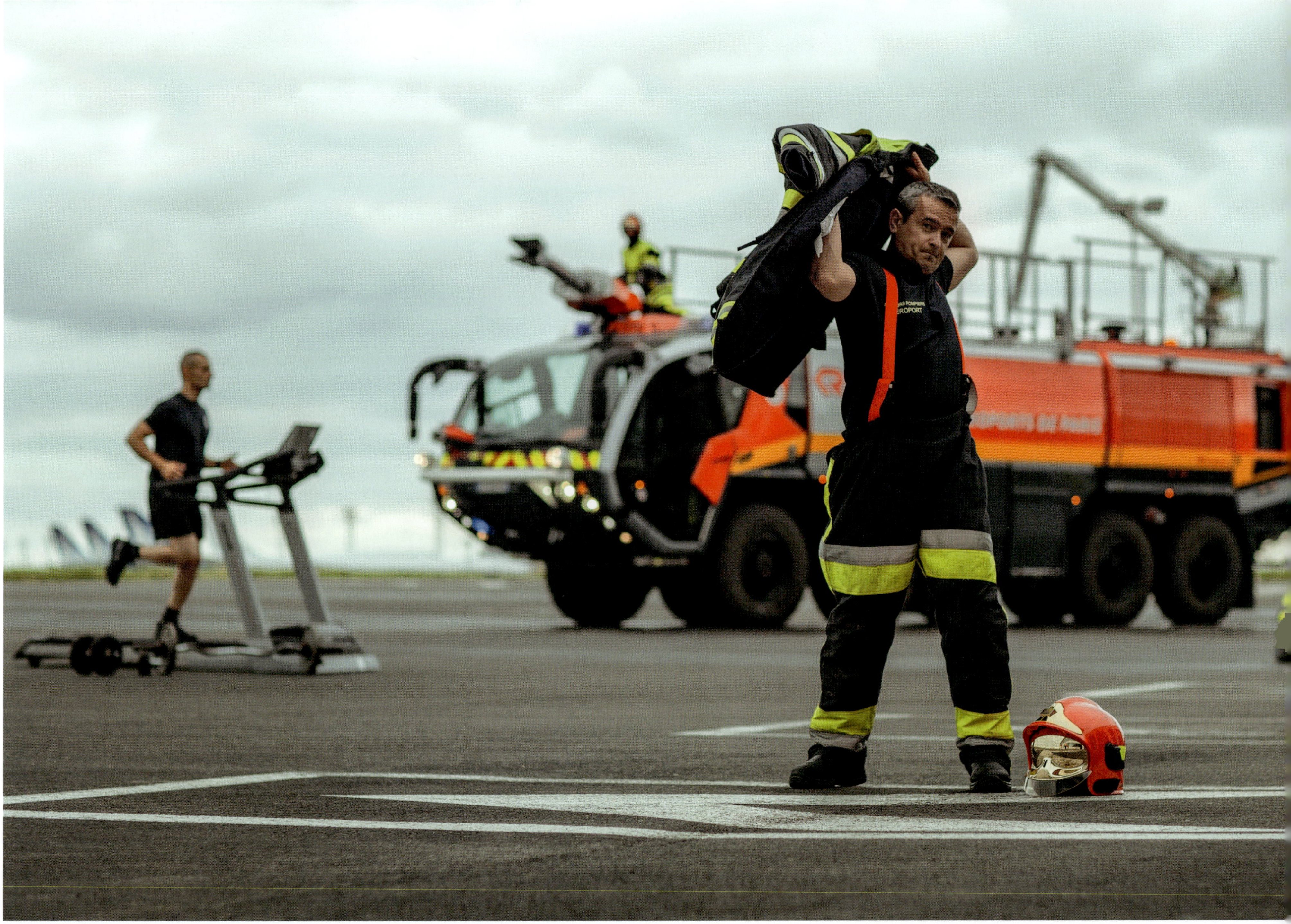

Left: Taken from the exhibition *Nos métiers ont du cœur* (Our skills have heart). Pictured are Bertrand, Daniel, Jean-Luc and Maurice.

Above: Taken from the exhibition *Regards en coulisses* (Looking behind the scenes). Caroline, the captain of an Air Caraïbes A330.

Using tractors to move planes on the ground could save billions in fuel. Airbus and Boeing have done the calculations. So far, the method is only used for positioning planes on the taxiways.

Taken from the exhibition *Regards en coulisses* (Looking behind the scenes). Seen here: Bruno, Air France.

The diameter of a Boeing 777 engine is roughly the same as the fuselage of an Airbus A320.

Taken from the exhibition *Regards en coulisses* (Looking behind the scenes). Seen here: Virginie, Corsair.

GEO-THERMAL HEATING

Since March 2011, Groupe ADP has used a geothermal plant to heat the Paris-Orly South and West Terminals, an initiative that confirms its commitment to the principles of the Grenelle Environment Forum. This ecologically sound heating is made possible by the availability of naturally hot water drawn from 1,800 meters below the surface. The Paris Basin is sited on the Dogger water table, a sustainable source of heat that was abandoned in 1985 when petrol prices fell after the petrol crisis. Groupe ADP has invested nearly 12.7 million euros in this geothermal installation. Apart from substantial economies in gas and fuel oil, geothermal power has cut Groupe ADP's CO_2 emissions by at least 8,000 tons per year.

The system is based on two wells, the first well extracting hot water at 74°C that passes to a heat exchanger and thence to the airport's central heating circuit. When the water has completed its circuit, the temperature has dropped to 35°C and is returned to the Dogger water table via the second well. This system supplies around 50% of the needs of Paris-Orly Airport and is very cost effective, with a price of five euros per mW/h compared to 30 euros for natural gas.

Concern for the environment is also behind the installation of two new-generation 19mW gas central heating furnaces, with two chimneys equipped to control atmospheric emissions. The network now also employs a low-temperature water circuit, and refrigeration too is three times more efficient than it was. Temperature control inside the West and South Terminals has also been optimized, with night-time ventilation in summer to reduce the need for air conditioning in the day. The Orly South airlocks have new insulation, and there's more conservative heating of the entrances in winter.

There's another innovation in the restaurant operated by the enterprise Orlytech. More than 650 meals are served here daily, which entails more than 5,000 liters of hot water every day. An 80m² photovoltaic system has been installed to supply the electricity for the huge electric heater that's needed here. This back-up system saves nearly 42% of electricity per year, equivalent to two tons of CO_2.

Geothermal heating was introduced at Paris-Orly in 2011 and will eventually cover half the cost of heating for Paris's second airport.

The Orlyval automatic shuttle connects the Antony RER station to the South and West Terminals.

The Orlyval station at the West Terminal of Paris-Orly airport.

View over the runways from the South Terminal.

First level of the South Terminal with its fast-food outlets.
The stairs at the back give access to the terrace on the next level.

CLOSER TO THE SKY

They work together in the public part of the South Terminal, just a few meters apart. They talk together every day, they know each other, and they share a mutual appreciation and respect. The chaplains of Paris-Orly represent one of the finest examples of inter-faith dialogue in France.

For Groupe ADP they represent a considerable asset. The rabbi, the priest, the imam and the pastor do not simply represent their faith, but also demonstrate sympathy and understanding. "We saw this after the attacks of November 2015," says Groupe ADP president-director general Augustin de Romanet. "The quality of the declarations between the different religions was far superior to the words spoken at a national level." After the Bataclan attacks, the Paris-Orly chaplains wrote a prayer for travelers, for all religions and in every language. That same solidarity was again expressed after the Charm el Cheikh attacks in Egypt in 2005, as the families of victims were received on their return.

For the Groupe ADP president, it is a considerable asset to have cultivated this tradition of respected chaplains and put it to good use. "The shock of these terrorist acts gave us the opportunity to demonstrate something that we already possessed, a spirit of fraternity," recalls Nadir Mehdi, one of the Paris-Orly imams. To illustrate this inter-religious fraternal spirit, Catholic chaplain Father Rodde borrows the words of Achille Ratti – Pope Pius XI – and his statement on the rise of fascism at the beginning of the 1930s. "We are all semites. Just a common trunk with different branches." Haïm Korsia, France's chief rabbi and a chaplain at the airport for many years, sees this as an extraordinary place for contact between people. Passengers in transit and airport staff come to the chapel, the synagogue or the mosque for advice, a discussion in calm surroundings away from the bustle of the airport.

The chaplains are also there to calm passengers who may be stressed. Some ask for a blessing before boarding because they are anxious. "In the middle of Ramadan, a man from the Ivory Coast came to ask me how he might break his fast in mid-flight. I told him that travelers were not obliged to observe Ramadan. It's a matter of advice, simple questions," explains Nadir Mehdi. "The people are happy to find us together, in a shared space," says Haïm Korsia. "We are there to listen to everybody," adds Pastor Anniel Aton.

These days at Paris-Orly it is not rare to see the chief rabbi of France come in person to ring the bells of the chapel. He even came to greet the Pope several years ago. At the airport, travelers speak more freely. "There's a greater confidence among the passengers than in other places, because these passengers know that they are not here to worship!" explains Haïm Korsia. With this happy co-existence between the representatives of different faiths, the chaplains of Paris-Orly are pleased to think that they provide an example for all of France.

As a beautiful illustration of this inter-religious co-fraternity, Paris-Orly in spring 2017 hosted an exhibition of paintings on the theme of the olive tree with the title "Man is like the tree in the field." On show were reproductions of canvases painted by Jewish, Christian and Moslem villagers living in Israel, who had no previous contact with each other. One day, several among them met each other in a neutral space. Little by little they learned to see each other, talk to each other, know each other and even respect each other, despite their differences of faith, culture and education. Their prejudices were eventually set aside and their fears evaporated. A painting workshop on the highly symbolic theme of the tree, and especially the olive tree, served as a demonstration of "doing something together".

It came to pass at Paris-Orly airport: four religions together under one roof, in the Paris-Orly South Terminal.

The boutiques on the international pier, the airport's most recent 12,000m² departure lounge.

The building is especially well lit, with large glazed bays that look out on the tarmac.
The 950 seats in the waiting area all have electric power points.

THE PARIS-ORLY OF TODAY IS THE PLACE FOR CORSAIR! IT'S OUR BASE, OUR PLATFORM, OUR CRADLE ... IT'S THE BELLY FROM WHICH EVERYTHING COMES, OUR WOMB! THIS IS NOT THE ORLY OF FORMER TIMES. THE AIRPORT HAS BEEN PROFOUNDLY TRANSFORMED. CHECK-IN AREAS, THE DEPARTURES AREAS ... OR INDEED THE ENTIRELY NEW INTERNATIONAL PIER. EVERYTHING HAS BEEN REVISED AND MODERNIZED. IT'S SUPERB!

Pascal de Izaguirre, Corsair director

Opposite page: The international pier boarding gates.

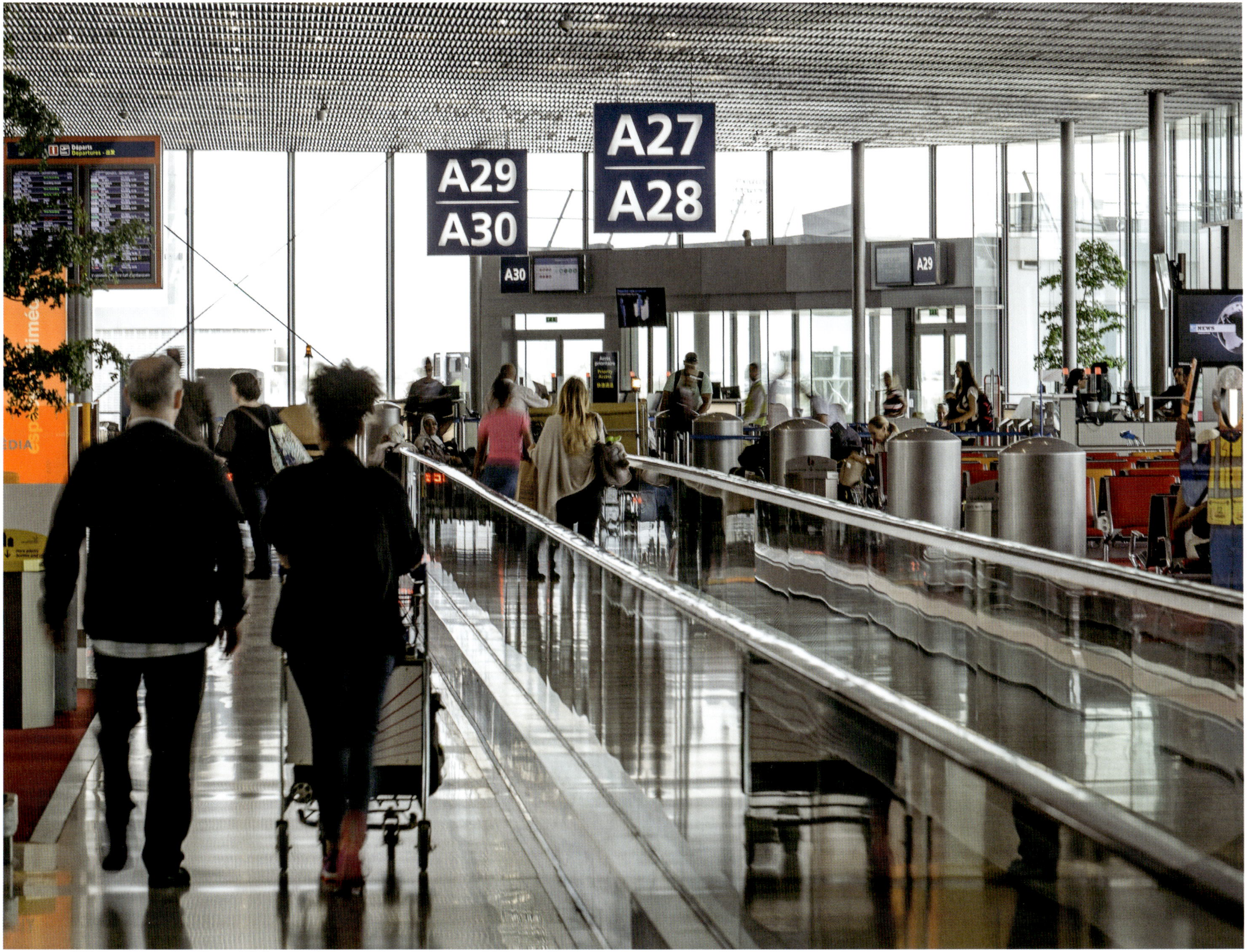
A29
A30
A27
A28
A30
A29

Hall 2 of the West Terminal, departure point for the Air France shuttle.

The upper level of Hall 2 of the West Terminal (arrivals).

Check-in desk and boarding in Hall 1 of the West Terminal.

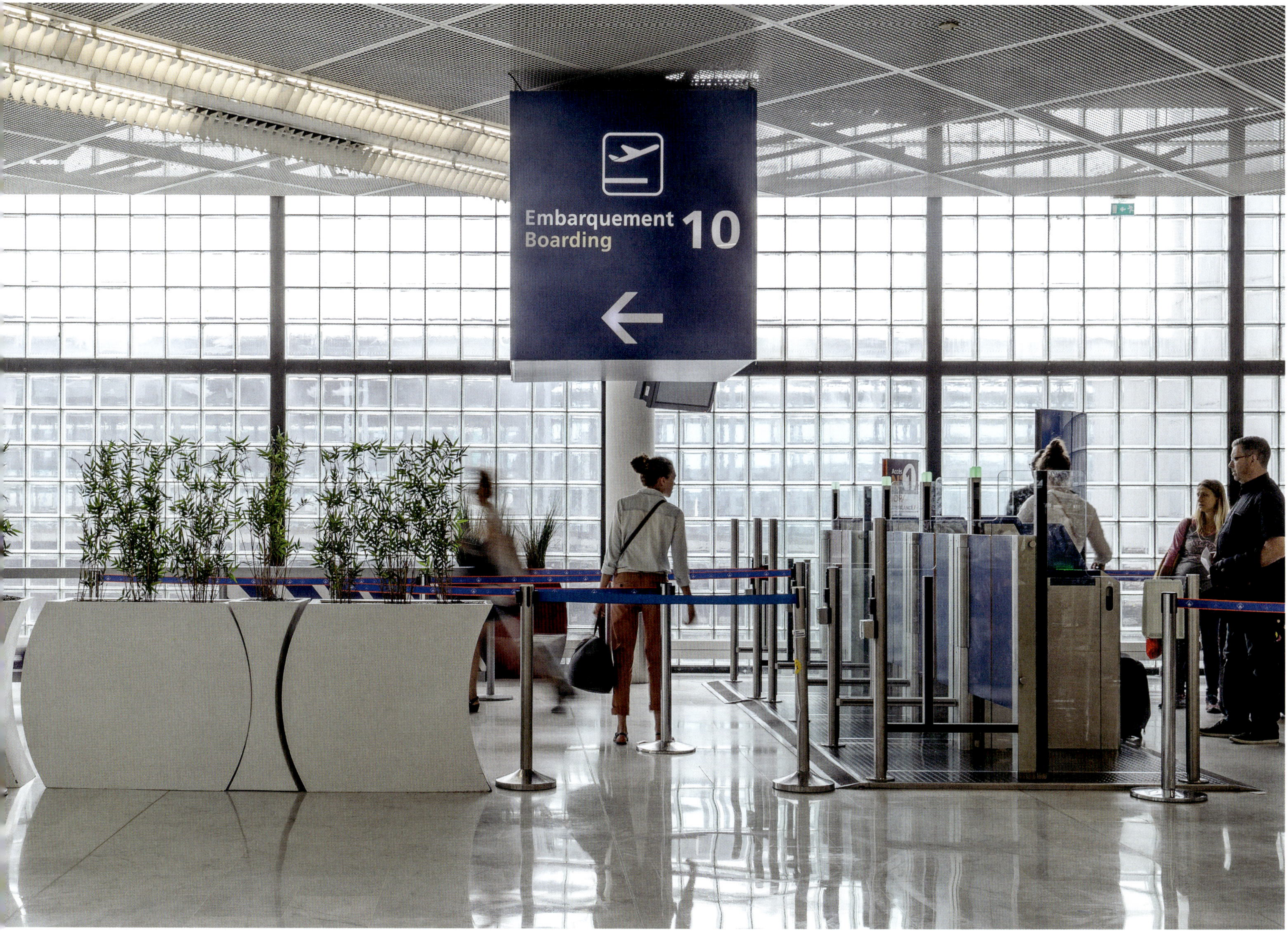
Embarquement
Boarding
10

PLANE SPOTTING

When weather permits, lenses in hand, they settle at the end of the runway, at Paris-Orly, Paris-Charles de Gaulle or Le Bourget, to scour the sky in search of a rare plane that they have never before recorded. These connoisseurs of a beautiful fuselage are the "plane spotters", an activity that sprang up with the Second World War and the Battle of Britain. Means of identification being very limited at that time, the government generally encouraged the practice, thus creating a sort of free, voluntary intelligence service. What could be more efficient than these enthusiasts who could describe at a glance all the features of an aircraft? Spotters would raise the alarm at the approach of German bombers.

In the United Kingdom they represent a historic heritage. People would come as a family to picnic around airports. There are in fact two kinds of spotter: those who go looking for a fine image to record, and those who collect registration numbers. The real enthusiasts are the English and the Dutch. It's a way to prove that they have seen thousands and thousands of aircraft. For these enthusiasts, every detail counts. Airlines work like the renters of cars. When they need planes, they rent the aircraft and apply their logo. The owner's brand mark is already there, which sometimes makes the plane a hybrid. The "real" spotters have reflex cameras with powerful lenses costing several thousand of euros. The most thorough even have little stepladders.

Several sites around Paris-Orly have been prepared for these spotters who come from all over the world. Overseas there are even travel agents who specialize in plane spotting, organizing guided visits to the great international airports with hotel rooms looking out over the tarmac – a paradise for these plane lovers.

After the attacks of 2001 and with the ever-present specter of the terrorist menace, the activity has been frowned on by the authorities. The situation has changed. Since 2006, plane spotting has become highly regulated and requires a permit from the authorities. Numerous associations such as Parisian Spotters represent these enthusiasts and process the authorizations. At Paris-Orly as everywhere else, the first priority is security. The gendarmerie carries out daily patrols, and a photographer without authorization is liable to a fine of 450 euros. But sanctions are rare, because serious spotters are valued as a source of warning. If something abnormal occurred, they would be the first to notice it and the first to warn the authorities.

Opposite page and above: Prototype Concorde 02 at the Athis-Mons Delta Museum by the side of the N2 highway – now retired for more than forty years.

Left: The American presidential plane Air Force One, carrying president Donald Trump on a visit to Paris, 14 July 2017.

Baggage hall on Level 0 of the South Terminal.

Using the latest systems, Paris-Orly can process 1,200 items of luggage per hour.

PARIS-ORLY: WHAT AN EXTRAORDINARY FUTURE AWAITS US ALL, WITH THESE HUGE CONSTRUCTION PROJECTS AND THE PLANNED CONNECTIONS BETWEEN TRAM, METRO AND TRAIN!
PARIS-ORLY: NO ONE WANTS TO AND NO ONE CAN REPLACE THE DYNAMIC IMPACT THAT THIS AIRPORT BRINGS TO THE FRENCH ECONOMY.

Marc Rochet, director Air Caraïbes — French Blue

Opposite page: The N7 highway runs under the runways and taxiways. The road is used every day by more than 120,000 motorists.

147

THE MARSH FILTER

Above: A pond and a marsh planted with reeds serve to extract the de-icing products picked up by the airport's rainwater. No other airport has a system like this.

Opposite page: The system is based on twelve ponds, each 500m², planted with reeds, bull rushes and iris.

In the autumn of 2013, Groupe ADP installed an innovative system for the filtering of run-off water: the Paris-Orly marsh filter. Dirty rainwater and contaminated water running off the runways and taxiways are treated in a marsh basin planted with reeds.

When it rains at an airport, the water washes the runways and carries off products used on the planes, such as the glycol used for defrosting the planes and de-icing the runways in winter, along with tyre rubber, oil and various hydrocarbons. Before 2013, the 3-5 million cubic meters of rainwater collected each year was entirely treated by the airport's Système de Traitement des Eaux Pluviales (STEP), managed by the company Suez. But in the coldest months of the year, when the operation of the airport required large quantities of glycol, these systems proved less effective. So in 2013, to complete the physico-chemical treatment, Groupe ADP invested nearly four million euros (20% financed by the Agence de l'Eau Seine-Normandie) to build 12 basins of 500m², planted with 36,000 reeds, bull rushes and iris in a bed of sand and ballast. This marsh filter was devised by subsidiary ADP Ingénierie (ADPI) assisted by the expertise and technical services of the Aviation Civile, working with a group of enterprises and the Antea Group design office. It was opened on 8 April 2014.

The bio-purification treatment works in two stages. Firstly, the run-off water is channeled to a holding basin of 13,000m³. Biomass (bacteria and vegetable matter) plus oxygenation degrades the polluting compounds in the course of 24-48 hours. Next the water is channeled to the marsh filter where it is cleaned by the sand, with the reeds serving to oxygenate this mineral filter. The system is entirely automated and computer controlled, and is the only one of its kind in Europe. Provisions are in place to handle the water as it leaves the marsh. If the water quality is good, it returns to the earth after passing through the STEP system. Otherwise it is returned for a second cycle of treatment by the marsh filter.

Groupe ADP always strives to improve the ways in which it manages environmental impact. This marsh filter allows on the spot treatment of run-off water by means of a self-contained system that respects the environment.

LA MAISON DE L'ENVIRONNEMENT

Paris-Orly and Paris-Charles de Gaulle each have a Maison de l'Environnement, for meetings and discussions, and to provide information and documentation to the public at large. The Roissy center was built in 1995, to plans drawn by Groupe ADP architect Michel Delpuech. The Paris-Orly center was built a year later.

These places present the history of the airport, explain how air traffic works and describe activities offered to passengers on the ground within the airport. There are frequent environmental exhibitions to explain the prevention and control of nuisances caused by air traffic. Former Orly air traffic controllers are always available to answer any visitors' questions. Local residents can view the trajectories and altitudes of aircraft for purposes of litigation.

The main role of these Groupe ADP-sponsored centers is to encourage better communication between the airports and local residents. They regularly hold meetings with the Commissions Consultatives d'Aide aux Riverains (CCAR) and are responsible for maintaining relationships relating to air traffic activity with the aid of the Autorité de Contrôle des Nuisances Aéroportuaires (ACNUSA). They also have a role to play in recruitment. Meetings are organized each year between professionals and the public to present the training available and skills required in the aeronautical area. The Paris-Orly Maison de l'Environnement is located on Rue du Musée, Athis Mons, to the south of the airport. It is open Monday to Friday. Entrance and parking are free.

Established at Paris-Orly in 1996, the *Maison de l'Environnement et du Developpment Durable* (MEDD, center for the environment and sustainable development) is at the heart of relationships with local residents and local elected representatives.

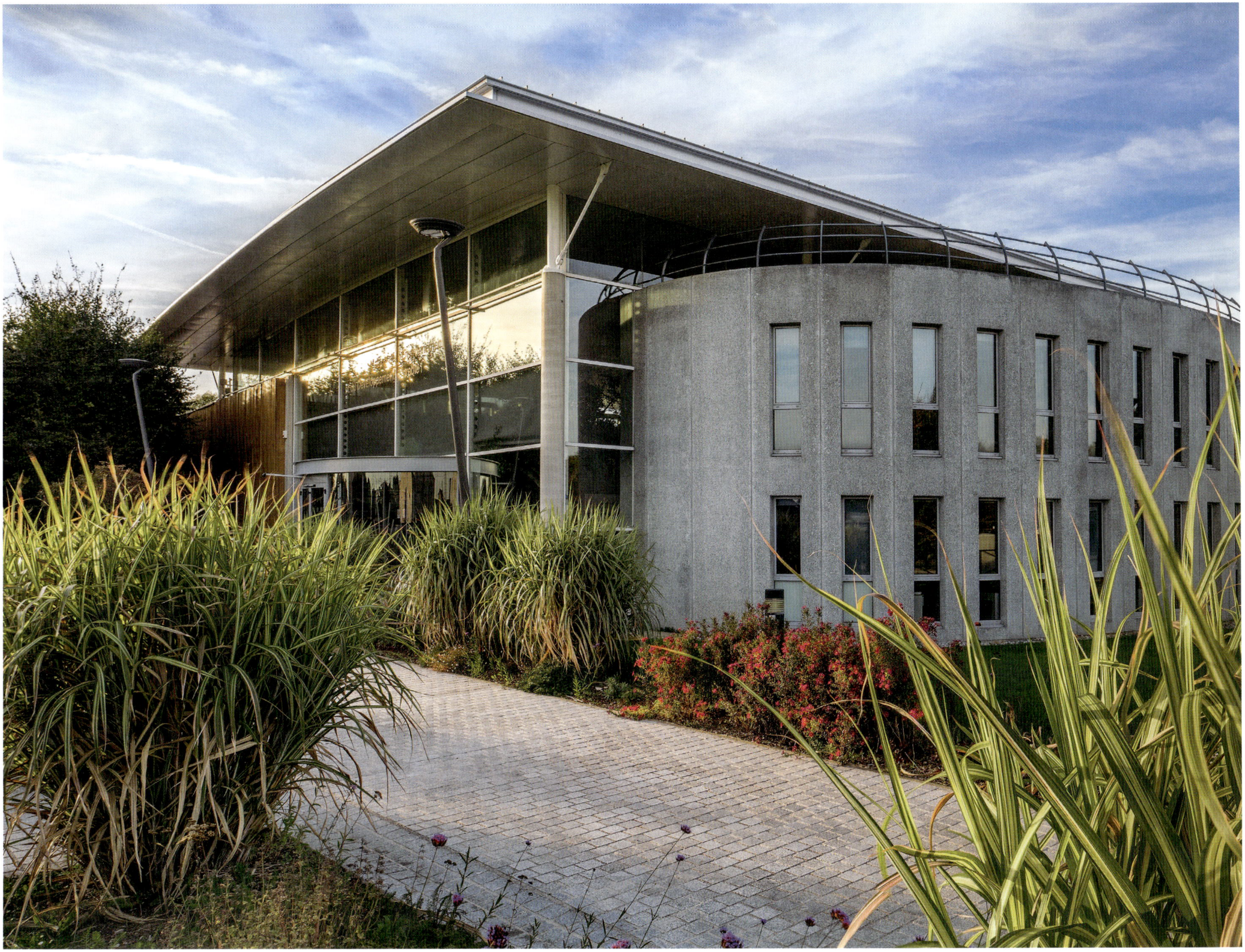

AN AIRPORT LOOKING TO THE FUTURE

A FRESH START

IN THE MIDDLE OF THE 1990S, PARIS-ORLY SUFFERED AN ATTACK OF THE BLUES.

It was abandoned by Air France, which was now entirely committed to its "hub" at Paris-Charles de Gaulle, and abandoned by many other operators – a trend made worse by the increasing strength of the TGV, which had progressively drawn passengers away from Orly's traditional domestic routes.

Franck Mereyde, director of Paris-Orly from 2011 to the end of 2017, recalls the circumstances. "Paris-Orly has experienced moments of difficulty. When Air France created a passenger hub, at the beginning of the 1990s, most international flights transferred to Paris-Charles de Gaulle. Since Air France represented nearly half the activity, from 1966 onwards this strategy turned Paris-Orly into a mainly domestic airport. At the beginning of the 2000s, substantial activity returned with Air Liberté, but the failure of this company several years later was a heavy blow."

Among other things, the disappearance of Air Lib in 2003 – the number two French air operator – left 3,200 staff unemployed, not counting the repercussions for subcontractors. This social dimension to the story forced the management of Groupe ADP and other players in the airline business to question the economic model for Paris-Orly, its position at the heart of the town and its long-term prospects.

Some political opinion even favored the pure and simple closure of the airport, a course of action recommended again as recently as 2011 by many members of parliament, among them Éric Woerth, David Douillet and Guy Malherbe, then deputy to former transport minister Nathalie Kosciusko-Morizet.

Starting in the 1970s with Southwest Airlines in the United States, low-cost airlines in Europe have changed the game and changed the shape of the sector. The de-regulation of air traffic authorized by Brussels in 1997 served to encourage the creation of these new companies. A lucky outcome for Paris-Orly. The pioneer was Irish Ryanair, but it chose to fly to secondary airports, like Beauvais or Charleroi in Belgium. That wasn't the way with EasyJet when it came on the scene in 1995.

The economic model was simple: one class, a reduced crew, a single fleet, a higher density of seating and, most important of all, point-to-point flights without regard for connections. By stages the EasyJet economic model moved towards "middle cost". Unlike Ryanair, EasyJet has not been afraid to position itself at the largest airports, even though the costs might be higher, with a progressively refined offer of the sort that would also attract the business market. This strategy has proved profitable, and has been followed by other carriers like IAG and its Spanish subsidiary Vueling, as also the Air France subsidiary Transavia that is developing a part-leisure, part-business profile. Most of all, this has created the opportunity to re-establish the appeal of Paris-Orly. In which respect, the curfew is no longer a problem and even an advantage, because it constrains operators to work towards a more and more rigorous punctuality.

As direction of the airport says: "Six o'clock in the morning to eleven o'clock at night – it's the optimum time period for the business market which aims to go there and back in a day. If punctuality is well managed, it's an excellent product. We are ready to turn constraints into benefits. If you compare Paris-Orly to Heathrow in London, for example, here at Orly we have no problem of runway saturation. Our focus is on simplifying the customer's passage through the airport, the checking-in of baggage, controls at security and immigration. We don't need seventy years to make the transit of the passenger smarter."

As to Paris-Orly's limited time slots, time has shown that with perseverance everything is possible. EasyJet started from nothing, with not one single slot. But the company today accounts for 10% of flights out of Paris-Orly. Another strong sign that the airport is once again becoming very attractive. Air France has decided to enlarge its short- and medium-haul offer with its subsidiary Hop, and in 2016 re-launched its route to New York.

Today, Paris-Orly is successfully re-established across Europe, and for international destinations too, with no loss to Paris-Charles de Gaulle. From that point on, this airport has been regarded with renewed interest.

No more talk of closure or relocation. With this renaissance came plans to spend 1.5 billion euros on a global modernization of the site. Such commitment had not been seen since 1971's opening of the West Terminal. The effects have been visible since 2015 with the opening of the pier to the east of the South Terminal. But the most impressive changes are yet to come.

After the opening of the walkway between the Cœur d'Orly business center and the South Terminal, the refurbishment of pedestrian spaces and the terminal esplanades, the transformation of the airport continues. Not far from Gate B, at the foot of the control tower, the focal project in the renaissance of Paris-Orly is the connecting building, cornerstone of the projects that represent the renewal of the airport. This is a project beyond the norm, partly for the size of the building and partly for the airport design logic that it represents.

This 80,000m² construction is going to link the South and West Terminals and reorganize them as a single terminal with four departure halls, in place of the two terminals and six departure halls that we see now.

Groupe ADP's 460 million euro investment here will raise Paris-Orly to the best level of passenger handling facilities in Europe, with new check-in points, new departure lounges and faster baggage sorting, entirely automated. Large spaces will have a human feel, including a huge wall of water more than nine meters high, luxurious finishes, a monumental work of art and nearly 5,000m² of shops to attract customers in a calm and peaceful atmosphere.

Simplicity, accessibility and practicality are the brief set for the construction of the building. Henri Vicariot's South Terminal will be conserved. Maybe its originally light blue ceiling has become more turquoise over the years, but the building was in its time very well conceived. Paris-Orly's main quality was always practical. There's no skimping on the investment. Again today, the major works pose no problems. The entrance airlocks will remain unchanged – they still open extremely well. The building has lasted better than many other great constructions of the 1970s. The other great quality of the South Terminal is the design of its spaces. Vicariot had a broad vision. With an occupancy that has more than quadrupled today, the grand hall on the ground floor still absorbs the flow of passengers without the impression that they are being trampled. What's more, the huge glazed facades provide a quality of natural light that adds to the charm of the spaces. The spirit of Vicariot is still present, in a style that blends modernity with the character of the original. It is not a museum, old things will go, but the soul of Orly will be preserved.

The soul and spirit of Orly are in its very clean lines, edges and angles, grand facades in glass and metal with no curves. Like Vicariot's terminal, the connecting building will feature grand facades and impressive ceiling heights – a deep building that all the same enjoys generous natural light, pleasant, functional and more ecologically sound. The new Paris-Orly will be much influenced by what has been done at Amsterdam Schiphol, which Franck Mereyde regards as a model. With the terminals joined, the names Orly West and Orly South will no longer make sense, and the choice of a new name is currently under discussion. This giant building 250m long with its 9,500m² of glazing will allow passengers to pass from the West Terminal to the South Terminal without ever leaving the airport. Car park signage will also be simplified to co-ordinate with the new halls.

In the international area, passengers will step out into a totally glazed walkway, with a panoramic view over the terminal. Land-side, you will see Paris, with the Eiffel Tower and the tower of Montparnasse in the distance. Air-side, you will be able to watch the coming and going of planes, and below too because the arrivals hall will be located on the terminal's highest level – a view that combines the life of the airport with a view of its departing passengers. Immigration will be located at the end of the walkway, for the sake of fluidity.

Eventually, Paris-Orly will become a fully multimodal transport hub, linking air, rail and road networks.

In 2024, just in front of the connecting building, this hub will incorporate a new underground station fully integrated within the re-planning of the airport, serving two Metro lines, the 14 and the 18. Paris and the Plateau de Saclay will be no more than 20 minutes from the airport. Line 14 connects with nearly 40% of the Ile de France in less than 40 minutes.

This double metro station will be one of the keystones in the transformation of Paris-Orly, located less than 50m from the connecting building and 500m from Terminus T7. All that's then missing is the TGV and the political will to extend it to the future terminal. In terms of infrastructure, the airport is already prepared for it.

"We are going to be the airport for the world of French research," enthuses Franck Mereyde. "With the Grand Paris Express metro, we will be just four stations from Villejuif, Europe's premier cancer research center, not far from the universities around Evry and, to the west, we would be directly linked to the Saclay hub which is now the base for nearly 15% of international research."

In this context, the Cœur d'Orly business complex represents a fabulous motor for economic development. Apart from the 28,000 jobs directly linked to the airport, the surrounding area with the Icade zone, the Belle Épine commercial centre and the Rungis market together account for 75,000 employees. Paris-Orly is part of a much more multi-faceted logic that addresses a multitude of different professions. "We are in course of creating a new town, with the good fortune to commence our projects alongside the projects for Greater Paris. This revitalization of Paris-Orly carries the whole region in its wake," says Franck Mereyde. The airport encourages the economic development of a region ready to capture global growth. To draw overseas businesses to the Cœur d'Orly business complex, Groupe ADP is thinking of building an international lycée. Paris-Orly has the chance to be hyper-connected to the rest of Europe. Orly is a better option for an overseas business than London, Barcelona, Rome or Berlin. But what makes the difference for a businessman who does not necessarily speak French is to know that he has the possibility of bringing up his children in an international framework. That's if he's not sufficiently attracted by the tourism, a certain French *art de vivre* and good eating. In 2024, it is expected that the Rungis market will feature La Cité de la Gastronomie, French cuisine represented in a place just two tramway stations from the airport. Paris-Orly stands

The connecting building between the South and West Terminals, in construction in September 2017.

Passengers disembarking via walkway at the Paris-Orly South Terminal.

at the heart of innovation, at the heart of research and at the heart of the menu also.

The airport is becoming a wired space, a real "Smart City", giving passengers the option to download a range of apps for entertainment – films, newspapers, games, photos, shopping – and equally a range of apps to handle check-in formalities, navigate the airport and communicate without constraint thanks to an automatic translator that works by voice recognition.

Soon a huge number of sensors and apps will be deployed to guide the flow of passengers in real time, regulating waiting times and security and adding to passenger comfort.

Groupe ADP's "Innovation Hub" program has already shown how the airport of tomorrow will work. The "Smart Airport" will be more and more connected.

Imagine how a future journey might go. Immediately before your arrival at the terminal, you have been geo-located and the airport software is automatically activated. As already happens today. The system knows from your last trip that you will be going home after your journey. It has allocated you a parking space if you have come by car, or else worked out the best transport option to get you to the airport. It finds your dossier number. You are already checked in. Cameras all around the airport have identified you by face recognition. So now Paris-Orly can offer passengers a personalized service that makes checks easier and improves security. You have agreed on previous visits that your profile can be recorded, so procedures are that much simpler. "Augmented reality" points you to the route you follow to deposit your baggage. On the screen of your smart phone, your route is mapped out across the floor. At the baggage point, a terminal simply requires you to scan on your screen the code of your "e-bag" that you previously registered at home. Everything is automated. Your baggage moves off on the conveyor belt, and you pick it up on arrival. Security is operating all the way, but it is less visible. You follow your path to the police checkpoint. This is the only time you have to show your passport, because every visitor is checked from arrival at the airport through to the departure gate. This is "hidden time" that actually allows you to gain time. "The technologies are in control, but it is important to be sure that there's no intrusion in people's private lives. Paris-Orly works today within the personal data protection rules of the CNIL: the information is gathered, processed and then deleted." The security barriers have gone. In the departure lounge you can enjoy the hall's various entertainments and services. Around you, walls of screens and projections invite your attention – a virtual cultural space, a cinema, an exhibition. Unless of course you prefer a spot of window-shopping. The boutiques have interactive screens and, if a product interests you, you can order it direct from your smart phone. It will be delivered to your home when you return from your journey. But now it is time to go to the departure gate. The app on your smart phone gives you a reminder and you follow the route on your screen right to the plane.

This futuristic but entirely realistic vision of tomorrow's airport-customer-passenger relationship has already sponsored the development of apps and services for the sharing of information between the administrator (the airport), the airlines, their ground staff and the air traffic services.

More than ever, roles within the airport are becoming digitized.

Since 2016, at Paris-Orly and Paris-Charles de Gaulle, the different participants in the airport arena exchange information for the purposes of "CDM" which stands for Collaborative Decision Making. Airport CDM is a project sponsored by the European Commission in association with Eurocontrol, with the aim of improving co-ordination across the different elements of airport management so as to free up the flow of traffic and improve decision-making. For example, the system can help an airline to find a passenger lost in the airport, to know whether or not they have passed through security, whether or not they are far from the boarding point. On that basis the airline can decide whether or not they should delay the flight by a few minutes and notify the air traffic services, or leave without the missing passenger. This information is shared across the airport chain.

Another example is in winter when the planes have to be de-iced. The de-icing of planes is today open to competition. When conditions deteriorate, at times of snow or a big freeze, a software app reports the number of aircraft needing treatment, the average time to do it, and the capacity of the services available to do it. With the materials for de-icing harmonized, if one operator is overloaded, he can get help from another operator who's there on site, the aim of course being that the aircraft should leave on time. Thanks to these new tools, the flow of air traffic improved by 10% in 2016 and the airlines' level of satisfaction with Groupe ADP has increased hugely to 86%. —

COMPUTE-RIZATION THAT HELPS EVERYONE

The computerization of airports makes life easier for passengers and introduces new solutions in the areas of safety, security, the movement of people and the working conditions of people on the ground. The «Internet of things» ushers in a whole new industry. Applications are without limit.

The Spanish start-up Think Big Factory proposes that in the near future the walls and floors of an airport lounge might become interactive, with various shopping options. In South Korea then at London Gatwick in the United Kingdom, they have tested the virtual grocery shop on the walls of the airport with the international supermarket operator Tesco. Using interactive screens, customers use their smart phones to scan the bar codes of the products they want to buy and have them delivered to their homes.

Based on this idea, New Delhi Airport has created its own shopping wall, offering luxury items, perfumes, jewelry, cameras and telephones. Companies like British Airways have experimented with digital label systems for luggage – personalized labels that are reusable and activated by smart phone. As to the end of queues at check-in desks, several initiatives give a glimpse of this evolution. With All Nippon Airways' Fast Travel program, for example, travelers are getting tablets for rapid check-in so they can then be guided from security control to the departure gate.

At London Heathrow and Frankfurt Rhein Main, iQueue is being used. This is a Bluetooth product that analyses the behavior of passengers and cuts waiting time. It observes the queues, the waiting time, the access controls and related services. This type of system will soon optimize the passage of the traveler through the airport.

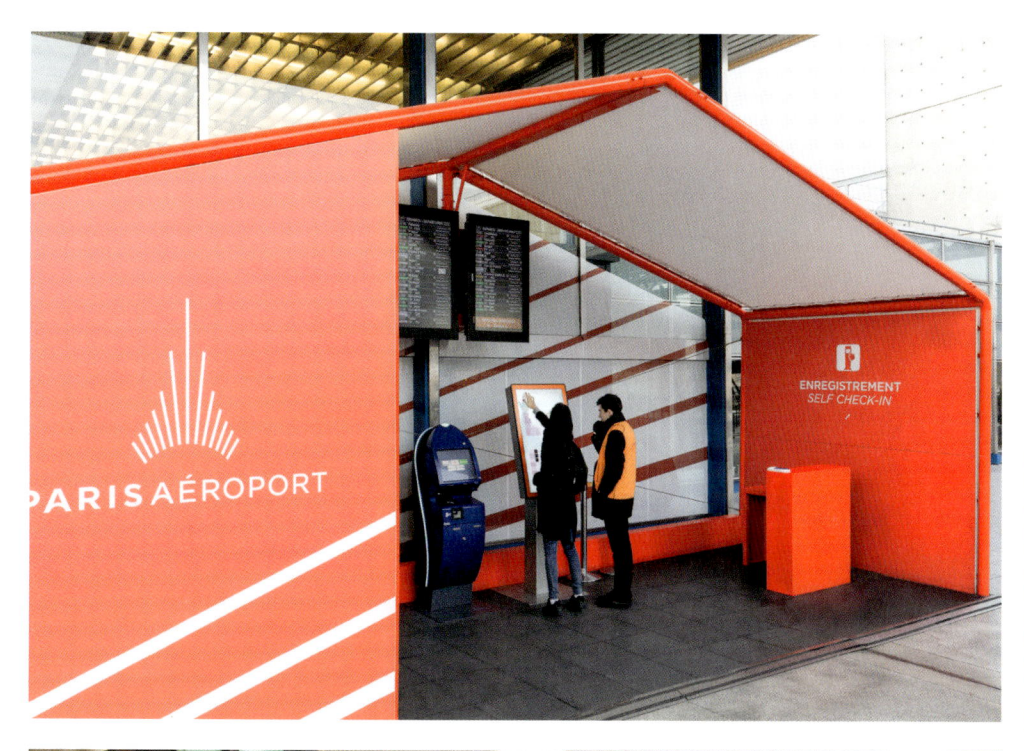

Left: Kerb-side registration terminal and information screens at the Paris-Orly South Terminal.

Below: The Paris Aéroport app gives users real-time information about traffic and the times of their flights.

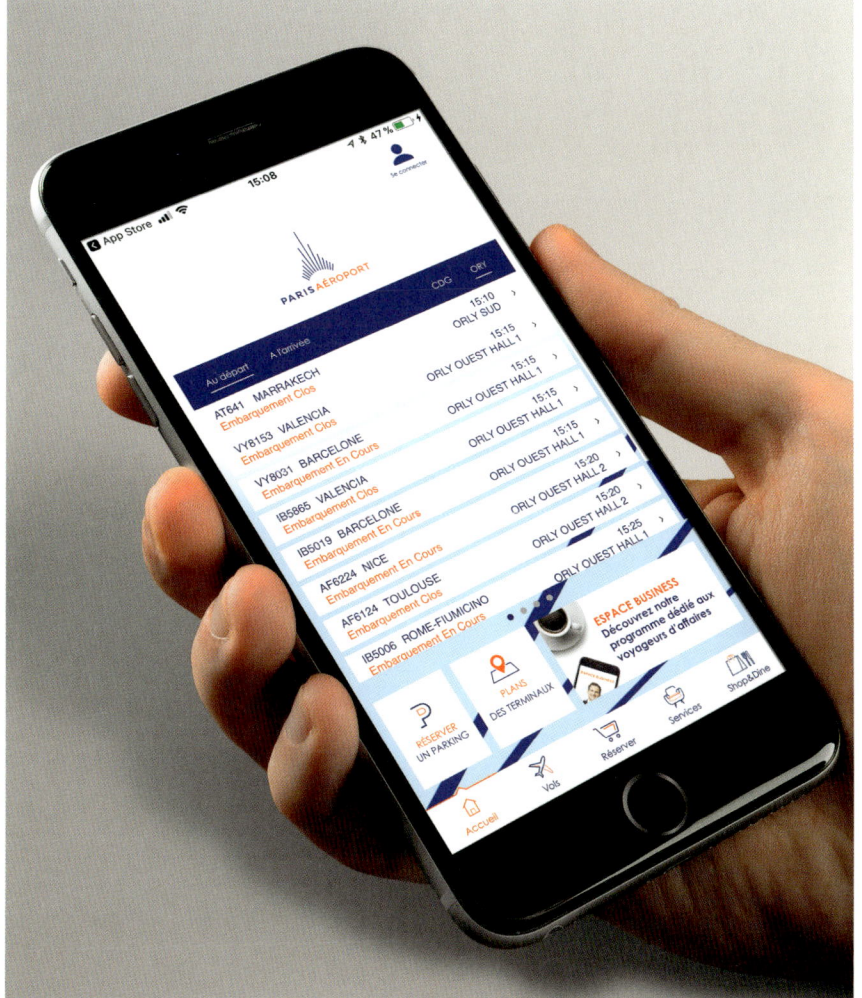

THE START-UP LOUNGE

This "connected space" is a free service for business travelers – a space for work, for relaxation and the opportunity to meet other professionals.

Thousands of businessmen, investors and start-uppers cross paths every day in the airports of France – without ever meeting. In 2015, in the middle of Hall 2 in the Orly West Terminal, close to the boarding gates, Groupe ADP created Business Space, a place to make connections, where passing businessmen, suppliers and the young newcomers of the digital world can meet and exchange, to expand their networks and forge relationships. Of the 9,000 travelers who come to this Hall each day, 58% are traveling for business reasons, 77% are senior managers, 86% are traveling alone.

The idea was born of a meeting between Groupe ADP president Augustin de Romanet and the president of Parrainer la Croissance, Denis Jacquet. Business Space is an area of about 40m^2 furnished with wide bench seating, several tables and a space apart for private discussions. The traveler identifies himself by connecting to the app My Airport in the area of the lounge and registers via Groupe ADP's own module or via his own LinkedIn profile. He then declares his presence as he enters Hall 2, and says he wants to meet other travelers. The space works by Bluetooth beacons fitted in the ceiling of the Business Space that geo-locate each person, and a message is sent to them via their smart phones. It's then up to them to accept or refuse the invitation.

This space offers a real opportunity for start-ups. Most are accustomed to promote their products, but that's mostly within their own ecosystems or in the company of incubators. It proves ultimately very difficult to expand their sphere of influence in the wider business world. Business Space was conceived as a bridge between the start-up world and the world of businessmen. It fills a real need, especially for those passengers with time to spare between two professional meetings. Encouraged by its success, the concept has been developed at Paris-Orly and Paris-Charles de Gaulle, where four further spaces have been opened.

A23
A24
BE MORE GOURMET
ARCADE
multimedia lounge
MULTIMEDIA LOUNGE
PARIS AÉROPORT

EasyJet is one of Paris-Orly's busiest carriers.

West Terminal first floor departure level.

PARIS-ORLY REMAINS AN EFFECTIVE PLATFORM, BOTH IN TERMS OF SERVICE TO PASSENGERS AND FLIGHT OPERATIONS. CIRCUITS ON THE TARMAC ARE SHORT AND AIRCRAFT TURN-ROUND IS QUICK, WHICH IS IDEAL IN ENVIRONMENTAL TERMS. THAT'S THE KEY TO SUCCESS FOR MODERN AVIATION AND LOW-COST CARRIERS.

Francois Bacchetta, director, EasyJet France

Opposite page: Aerial view of Paris-Orly airport in April 2017. Construction of the connecting building has begun.

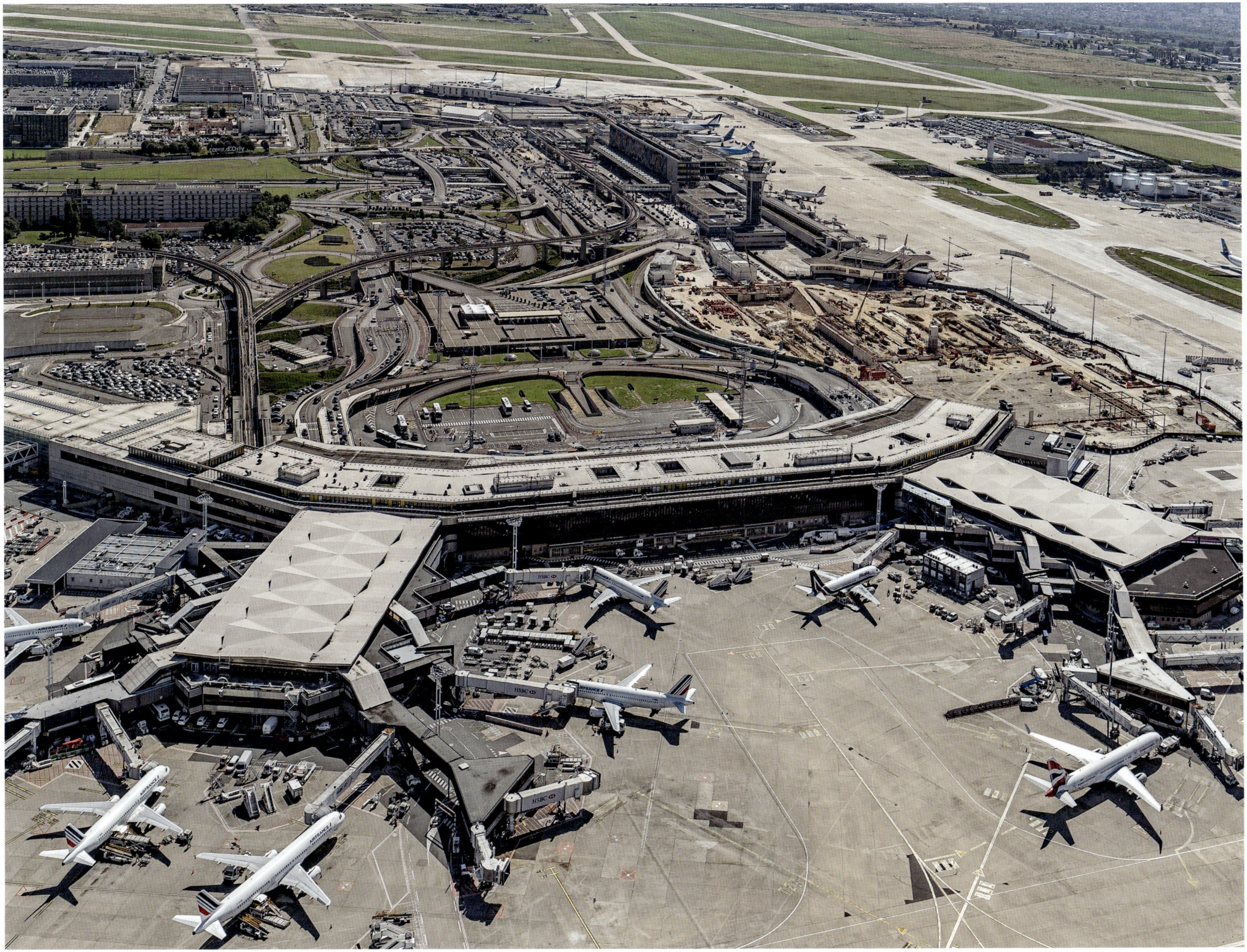

ARTPORT

To attract new business, passengers need reasons to prefer a change of flight in Paris, not London, Frankfurt or Amsterdam. With this in mind, Groupe ADP is capitalizing on the cultural image of France and its capital city.

The Espace Musées (museum space) is an unexpected and unusual cultural showcase that opened in 2013 in Hall M of Terminal 2E at Paris-Charles de Gaulle. The idea was dreamed up by Francis Briest, official auctioneer and co-president of art dealers Artcurial, in collaboration with former Groupe ADP number two François Rubichon. The idea is to offer a free exhibition of emblematic works from the great Parisian institutions, museums and foundations, in a display that changes every six months. This space has already hosted exhibitions devoted to Picasso, Rodin, Dubuffet, the Palace of Versailles, Sèvres china and young modern artists. It's an "art bubble" that serves to distinguish the airport on the world scene, offering a space that's made for relaxation and discovery.

Paris-Orly also hosts temporary exhibitions, presentations of ephemeral works and concerts. In 2015, the facade of the South Terminal acquired a monumental mural, one of the largest in the world, 200m long, 17m high, with an area of 3,200m^2, designed by Jean-Charles de Castelbajac. With a few pencil strokes, this fashion designer tells the stories of the lives lived by passengers and staff at the airport – stories that the artist found on the Internet. "An engaging study of the emotions of travelers, and a crystallization of the space-time that is the no-man's land of the airport," explains the artist.

In September 2018, the arrivals passageways of the South Terminal's Hall B are set to present a pictorial tour of French songs from the 1950s to the present day. This exhibition titled "French Pop" will gather together some 20 photographs of singers and composers like Jacques Brel, Johnny Hallyday, Serge Gainsbourg, Daft Punk, Stromae and Jacques Dutronc. *Paris Match* is sponsoring the pictures.

Exhibitions of artists such as Jean Jullien, Yanidel and Vincent Bourilhon have also been presented at the terminal.

Since 2016 in the summer period, Paris-Orly has also collaborated with the magazine *Les Inrockuptibles* to present a number of French-label artists in the context of the Paris-Orly Festival, the Paris Airport Music Workshops, and the Gate Up contest – an encouragement to inspiration and imagination that gives young artists a unique opportunity to perform in the heart of the airport. At the close of this concert series, passengers name the artist they liked best, who then gets to play at the Paris-Orly Festival.

THERE'S THIS MYSTERY, A TIMELESS CRYSTALLIZATION, A FEELING OF TRAVELLING FOREVER WITHIN THE AIRPORT. THE FORCE OF ORLY SOUTH IS THE FORCE OF MEMORY, OF THE 'SIXTIES WHEN I OPENED MY IMAGE-HUNGRY YOUNG EYES TO THE NEW WORLD. THE WORK OF HENRI VICARIOT IS PALATIAL. I ADORE ITS GREAT GALLERY OF MIRRORS, ITS TERRACES AND ALL OF THE POETRY THAT RADIATES FROM THIS SENSATIONAL GATEWAY TO THE SUN.

Jean-Charles de Castelbajac, artist

Opposite page: Second edition of the Paris Aéroport Festival staged at Paris-Orly on Saturday 14 October 2017.

Far left: The exhibition *Carte blanche à Jean Jullien*, artwork named "Where Did All the Fun People Go?" and "Concert" in the arrivals passage of the South Terminal international pier, Paris-Orly, August 2017.

Near left: Jean-Charles de Castelbajac in mid-creation in the Paris-Orly South Terminal.

In 2015, Groupe ADP engaged Jean-Charles Castelbajac to gather the experiences of passengers at the airport, and transform their stories to super-sized drawings. Stories of finding friends and partings, anniversaries, marriage proposals, all transformed to a monumental work of art that has for some time decorated the facade of the South Terminal.

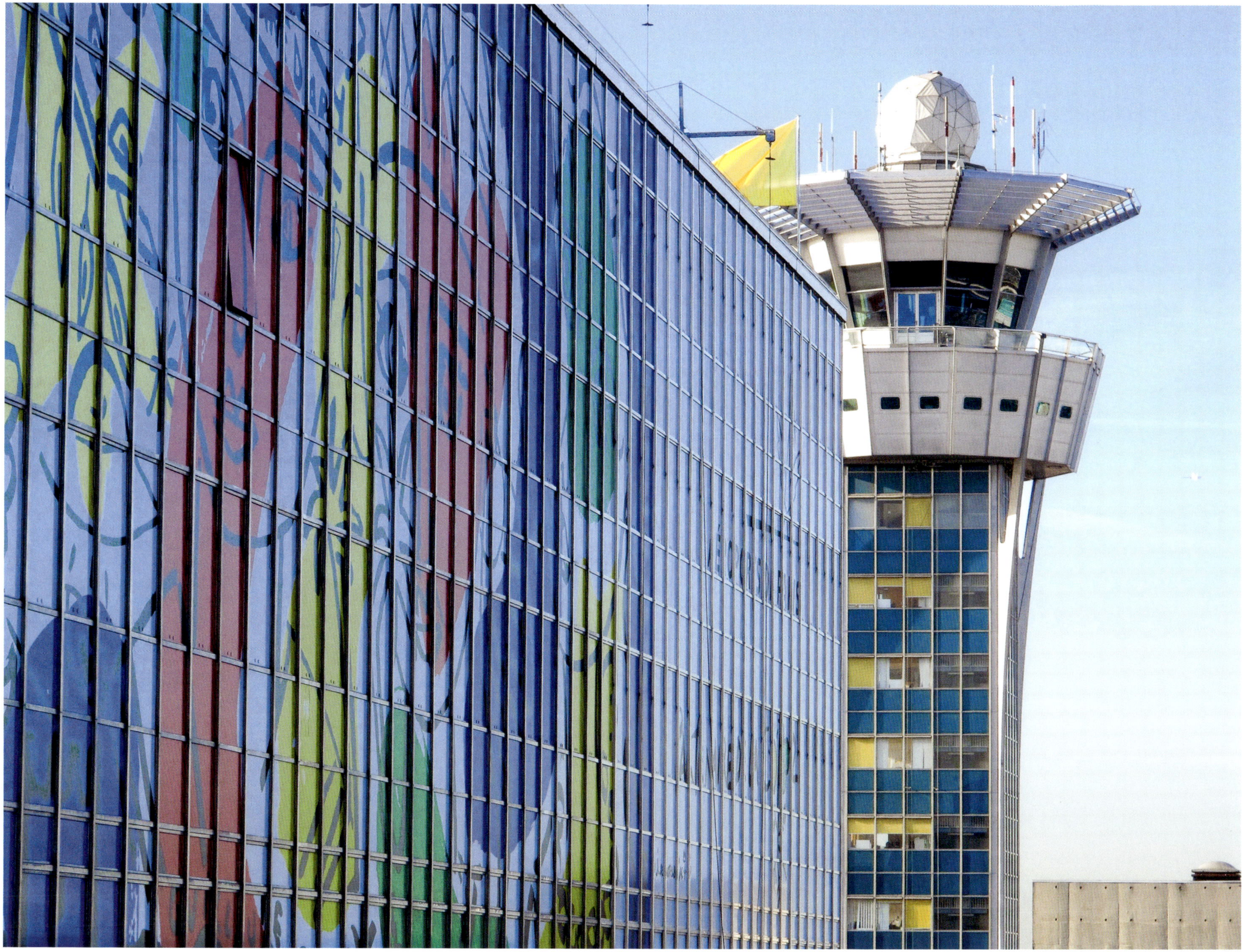

THE VASCO 3D TOOL FOR OPERATIONS MANAGERS, THE PRIMA MOBILE TOOL FOR CUSTOMER ADVISORS, THE BUSINESS SPACE CONCEPT AND MUCH ELSE — PARIS-ORLY HAS PROVIDED THE GROUPE ADP WITH A FABULOUS LABORATORY FOR INNOVATIONS. THIS IS WHERE WE ARE LAYING THE FOUNDATIONS FOR THE SMART AIRPORT, WHICH FROM 2019 WILL START TO TAKE SHAPE IN THE ALL-NEW CONNECTING BUILDING.

Edward Arkwright, executive managing director, Groupe ADP

Opposite page: Site of the connecting building, at the start of 2017.

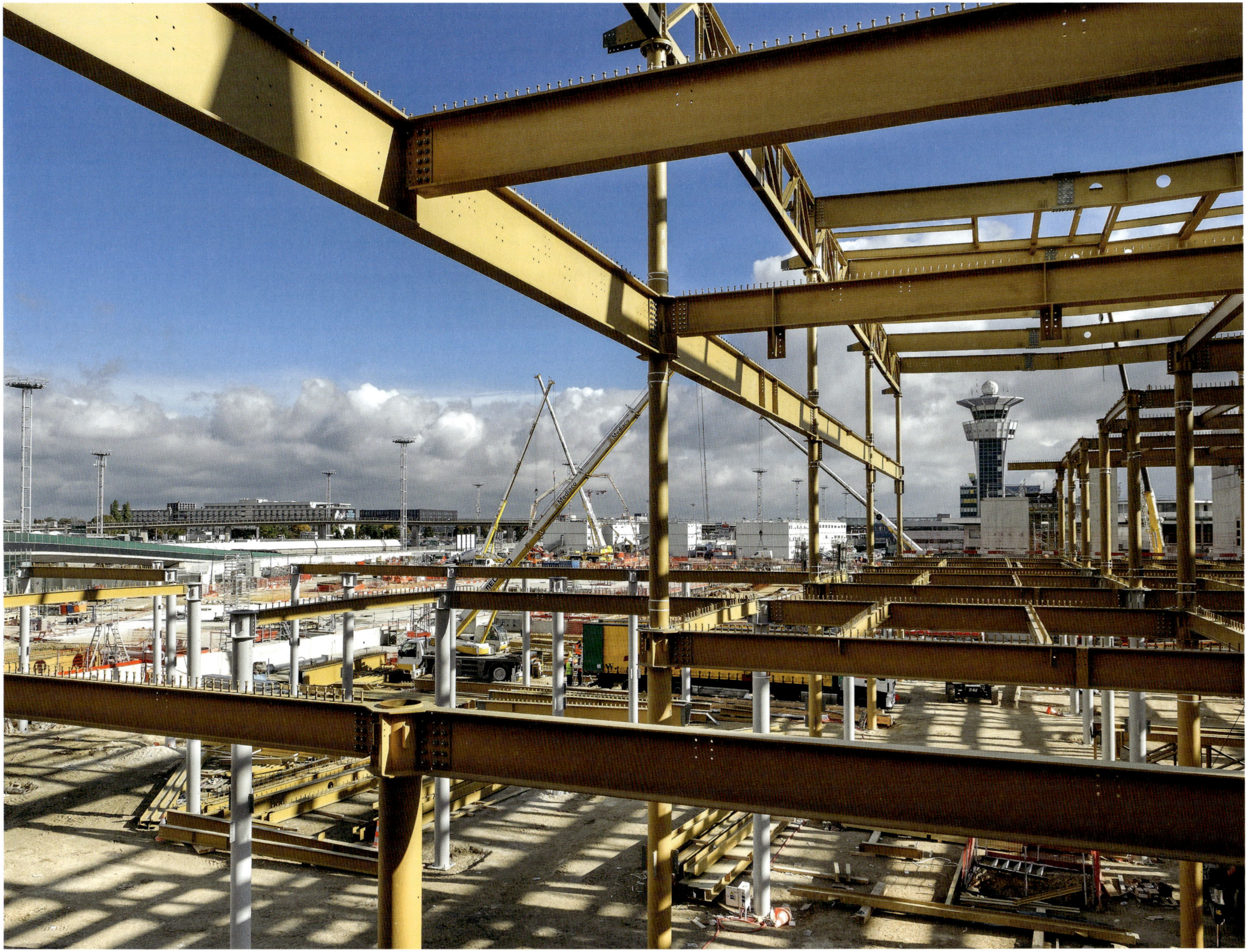

THE AIRPORT OF THE FUTURE

In March 2017, Groupe ADP launched a program called "Innovation Hub" as a means to explore the airport of the future. A 300m^2 space inside ADP's Paris-Charles de Gaulle headquarters is set up to receive the most creative start-up businesses. The Group aims to trial some fifteen projects each year and keep three or four – an experimental approach that comes from the digital world, far from the style of traditional aero engineering. The space is like the "fablabs" that have sprung up in the industry. "We have worked with start-ups for many years, but the idea this time is to do it in a concentrated fashion," explains Groupe ADP executive director general Edward Arkwright.

Innovation Hub represents a more structured response to the challenge of modernization in an increasingly competitive environment. Several projects have already been selected to go forward, like the robot valet parking system developed by the start-up Stanley Robotics and already operating at Paris-Charles de Gaulle Airport. The robot collects the car from a dedicated bay within the parking area, then deposits it accurately in a standard parking space – a solution that can increase parking density by 30-50%. Another start-up, Safety Line, aims to optimize the trajectory and speed of airliners on take-off, producing a potential 15% fuel saving. Innovation Hub is supported by a fund with 16 million euros to invest over five years. Groupe ADP's innovation budget is increasing by 3-4 million euros each year.

Opposite page:
The connecting building between West and South Terminals.

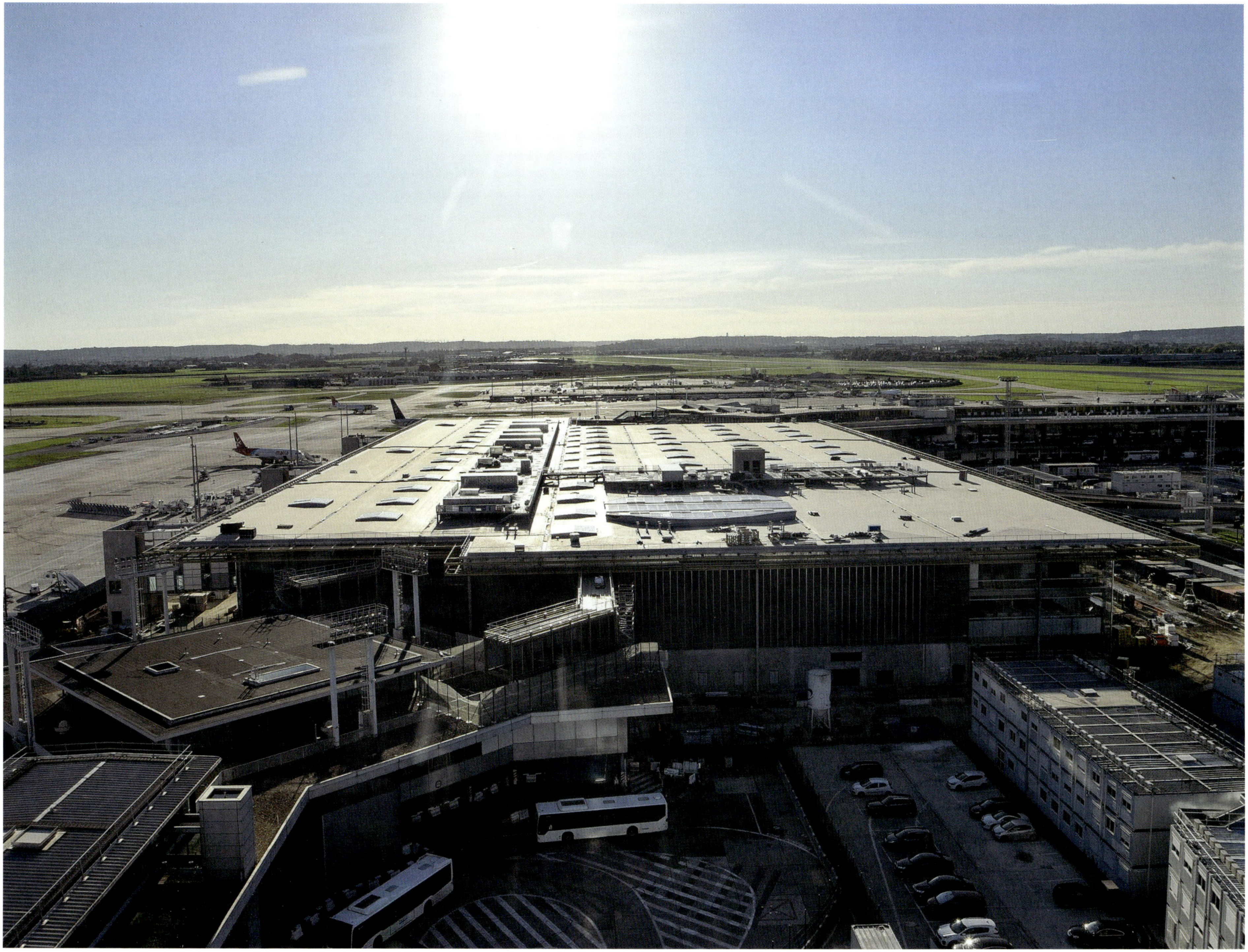

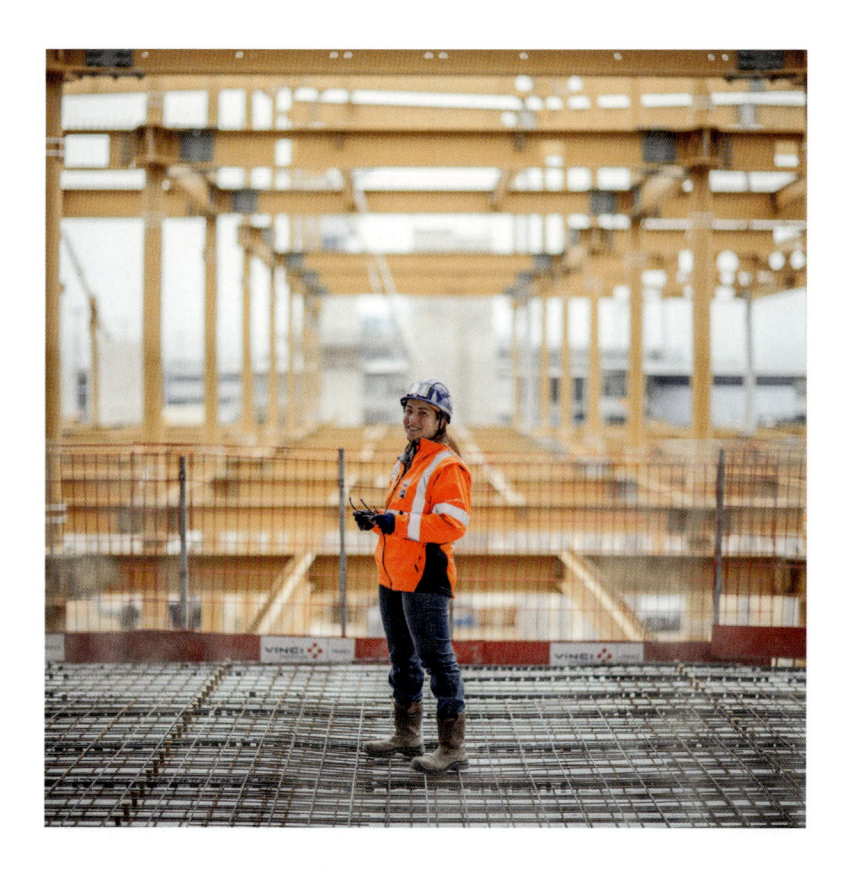

Above: The connecting building takes shape. It will open to the public in the first quarter of 2019.
Taken from the exhibition *Regards en coulisses* (Looking behind the scenes).
Pictured is Laetitia of Vinci Constructions.

Right: The connecting building represents a considerable extension of Paris-Orly's South and West Terminals
– an extra 80,000m² for the benefit of passengers.

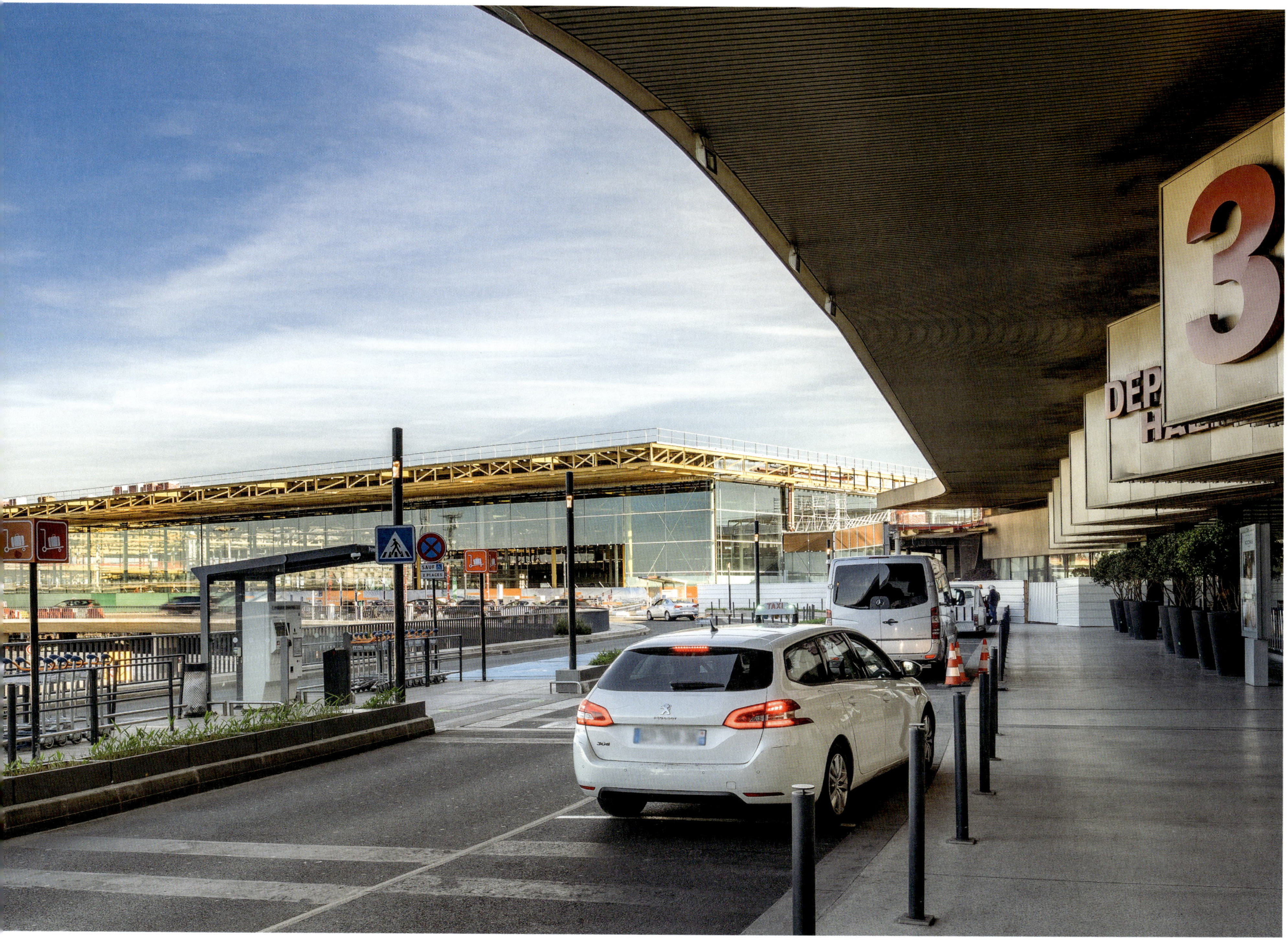
DEP
3
TAXI

WHAT WE ARE CREATING HERE IS A NEW TOWN, AN "AIRPORT CITY" AROUND PARIS-ORLY AIRPORT. WE ARE FORTUNATE THAT OUR PROJECTS ARE STARTING AT THE SAME TIME AS THE DEVELOPMENT OF GREATER PARIS. THE REJUVENATION OF ORLY IS DRAWING THE WHOLE REGION IN ITS WAKE.

Marc Houalla, director, Paris-Orly

Opposite page: Work progressing on the connecting building, viewed from the tarmac, Summer 2017.

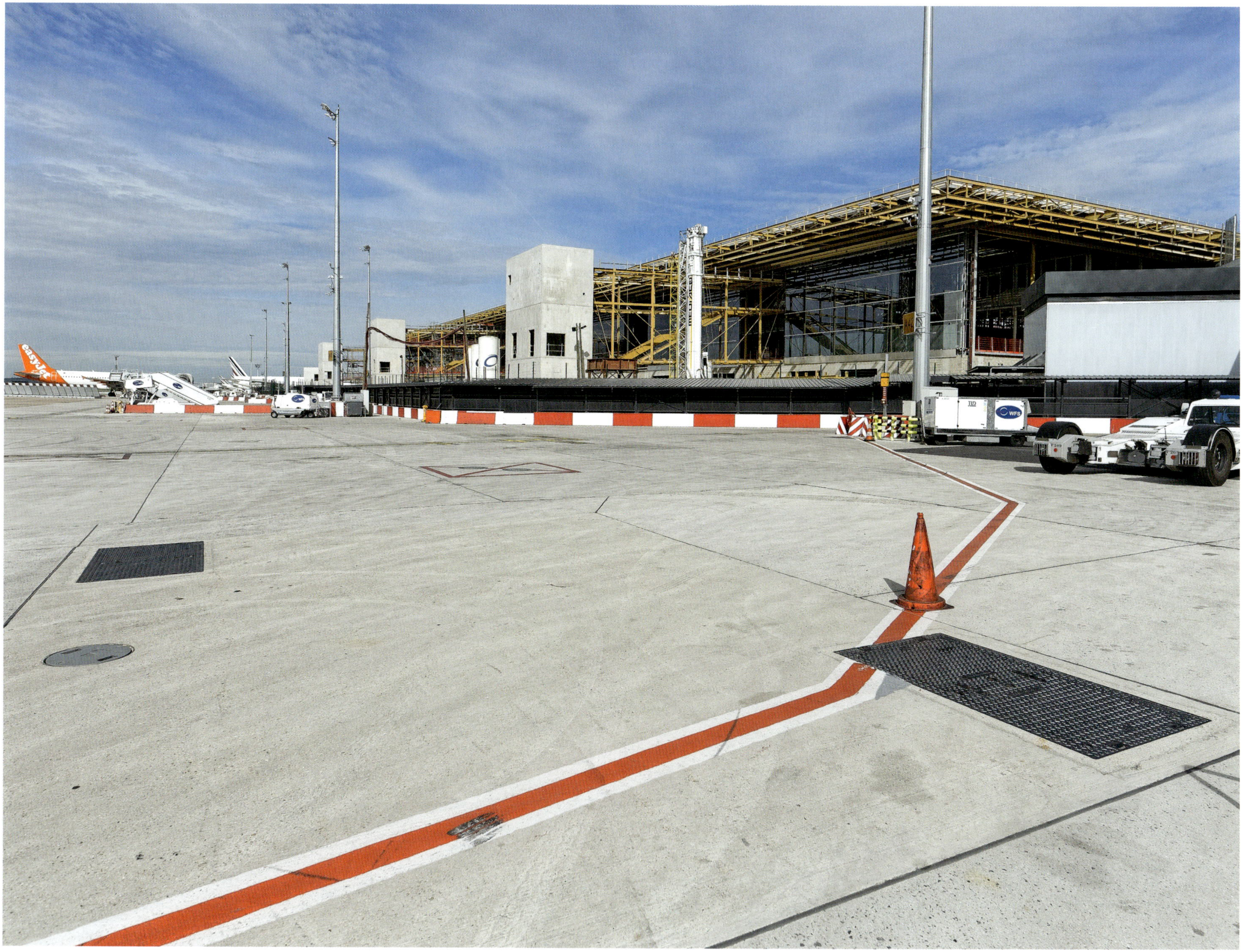
WFS

CŒUR D'ORLY

Cœur d'Orly is one of Groupe ADP's keynote projects – an energy-efficient international business center of 170,000m², immediately opposite the South Terminal, opened in 2007. Development was financed by Groupe ADP, Altarea, Cogedim and real estate investors Foncière des Régions. It comprises 70,000m² of offices, a conference and exhibition centre, a shopping and services complex and several hotels, including a four-star hotel, a Novotel and two Ibis hotels. The hotel element was financed by the Accor Group. The first building designed by Jean-Michel Wilmotte was opened in 2015. All parts of the development use renewable energy, geothermal and solar. The quarter as a whole is built to meet the requirements of the NF HQE certification for commercial buildings and BBC Effinergie.

Orly is the premier economic complex of the South Paris region, and Cœur d'Orly exists to enhance its appeal as a place for business and research, and a meeting point with a global reach. Beyond the airport, synergies will be developed with the nearby Rungis MIN (Marché d'Intérêt National), presently in course of renovation, with the future Cité de la Gastronomie and the Rungis enterprise park Icade, formerly Silic.

A 200m mechanized walkway connects the South Terminal to Cœur d'Orly. Thanks to its travelators, you can reach the airport, the commercial areas and the hotels in just seven minutes, compared with 15 minutes by car. This metal and glass structure built of 800 tons of metal and 200 tons of glass stands as a work of art in its own right, a technical and architectural triumph by two French suppliers, Vallourec for the steel tubes and Baudin Chateauneuf for the construction.

Paris-Orly enjoys the considerable advantage of a location entirely inside the perimeter of Greater Paris. Between now and 2024, the automatic Metro lines 14 and 18 will run from the airport to the centre of Paris and the Plateau de Saclay, Europe's Silicon Valley, in less than 20 minutes. It then remains to build the South interchange for the Atlantique and Sud-Est TGV services, expected beyond 2030 with a station at Orly. Right now, Cœur d'Orly is connected to the T7 Tramway, with a dedicated station for the purpose. The appeal of this energy-efficient business quarter is sure to grow and will maybe come to compete with the grand towers of La Défense. Some 15,000 jobs will eventually be created here.

The Askia building, designed by Jean-Michel Wilmotte.

Aerial view of Cœur d'Orly, Summer 2017.

Walkway creates a pedestrian connection between the Paris-Orly South Terminal and the energy-efficient business center Cœur d'Orly.

MODERN, ATTRACTIVE AND WITH A FOOT IN THE FUTURE, IT HAS RISEN IN THE OPINION OF THE COMMUNITIES AROUND IT AND IN TERMS OF BIODIVERSITY. PARIS-ORLY IS NOW AN AIRPORT TOWN AT THE HEART OF INNOVATIVE PROJECTS THAT ENJOY THE FULL SUPPORT OF LOCAL GOVERNMENT.

Christine Janodet, mayor of Orly
and a Val de Marne department council member

Opposite page: The Greater Paris station project, at the center of the Paris-Orly terminals.

183

PARIS-ORLY AIRPORT IN FIGURES

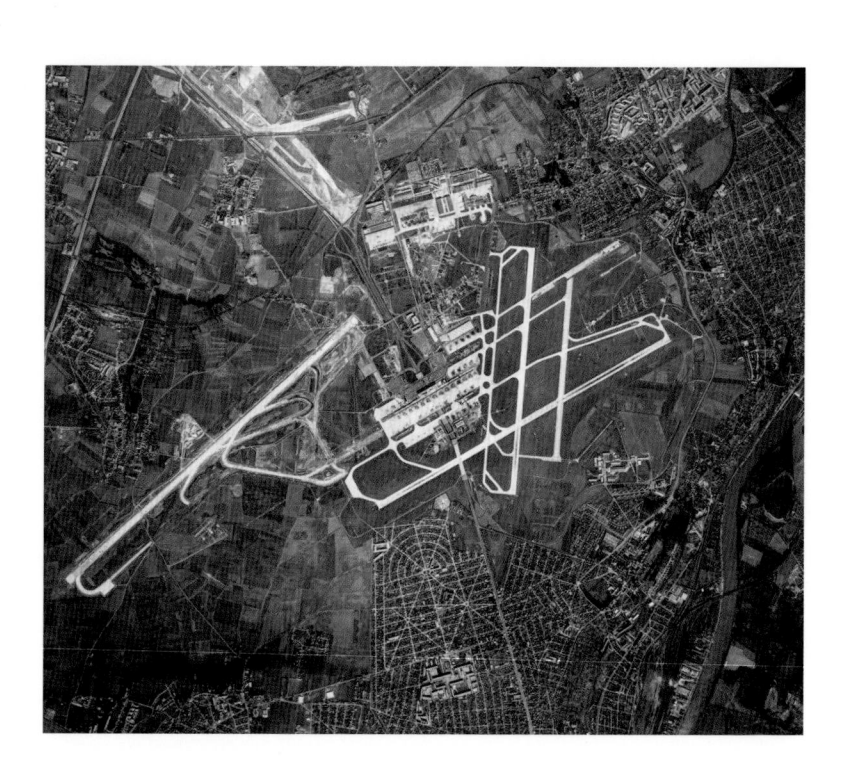

1
Number One airport inside the town, just 10km south of Paris, with a journey time less than 15 min

30,000
direct employees

Airport activities

2nd
airport in France

12th
airport in Europe

154
destinations served in 2016

2
terminals

3
runways

Up to 76
movements per hour

234,453
movements in 2016

80
spaces for landed aircraft

31.3m
passengers in 2016

184

KEY DATES

1909
Opening of Port Aviation airport with a dozen flying fields, including the site of the future Orly on the Longboyau plateau.

1918
Orly becomes an airport and an air base for the Americans. Requisitioned by the Germans in the Second World War.

1945
The company Aéroports De Paris is formed, with responsibility for the management of Orly and Le Bourget.

1952
Air France moves from Le Bourget to Orly. Orly airport handles 1.2 million passengers a year, twice the number at Le Bourget.

1954
Orly becomes an entirely civil airport.

1959
Air France baptizes its first Caravelle at Orly airport.

1961
President Charles de Gaulle opens the South Terminal, designed by architect Henri Vicariot. The tourists come in crowds, and Gilbert Bécaud sings *Les Dimanches à Orly*.

1962
Orly airport attracts more visitors than Versailles (3.4 million). The great stars of screen and music hall pose for photos on the plane stairs.

1965
Opening of the Paris-Nord airport at Roissy on 22 June. By the end of the year, the number of passengers passing through the Orly South Terminal is close to six million.

1966
Four million visitors come to Orly South to take lunch and stroll on the terraces, to watch the aircraft taking off and landing. The Orly control tower enters service. Start of Terminal 1 construction at Roissy-Charles de Gaulle.

1968
First telescopic walkways for the large planes. Orly airport proves it can adapt to the age of jets. Work started on the building of Orly West in October of the previous year.

1969
The Orly South Terminal reaches the 9 million passenger mark, half as much again as its theoretical capacity. The jumbo jets arrive (first landing of a Boeing 747 at Orly). Traffic passenger grows by more than 15%.

1971
Orly West Terminal, designed by Henri Vicariot, opens its doors following 40 months of work.

1973
Design starts on Terminal 2 at Roissy-Charles de Gaulle, even before Terminal 1 is open.

1974
The opening of Roissy-Charles de Gaulle airport, with its revolutionary terminal based on a cylindrical central core and seven satellites.

1986
Hall 4 at Orly-West is opened.

1987
Opening of the Orlytech commercial zone. The following year, Aéroports De Paris passes the 40 million passenger mark. Traffic has doubled in the space of eleven years.

1989
The name "L'Aéroport de Paris" is formally changed to "Aéroports de Paris" (by decree dated 4 January).

1991
Opening of the Orlyval rail shuttle, carrying more than 2 million passengers per year.

2012
Presentation of a grand modernization plan for Paris-Orly airport, looking forward to 2018.

2013
Start of work on the Cœur d'Orly complex – a keynote urban development project for Greater Paris. Cœur d'Orly will be an energy-efficient international business centre.

2014
The Paris-Orly "marsh filter" goes into service – a system unique among airports, for the treatment of run-off rainwater.

2015
Start of work on the connecting building.

2017
Opening of the walkway connecting the South Terminal to Cœur d'Orly.

2019
Paris-Orly airport will become more than just one unique terminal.

185

The Paris-Orly control tower.

AUTHOR FRÉDÉRIC BENIADA AND GROUPE ADP WISH TO THANK THE FOLLOWING FOR THEIR HELP

Jean-Marc Janaillac, president and CEO of the Air France-KLM Group; François Bacchetta, director, EasyJet France; Pascal de Izaguirre, Corsair director; Marc Rochet, director Air Caraïbes – French Blue; Nathalie Stubler, director Transavia France; Patrick Gandil, CEO of the Directorate General for Civil Aviation; Augustin de Romanet, president-director of Groupe ADP; Edward Arkwright, executive managing director, Groupe ADP; Franck Mereyde, deputy CIO, TAV Airport; Étienne Vicariot; François Dussurget and Vital Ferry of the journal *Icare*; Laurent Bailleul and the Association Anciens Aérodromes; artist Jean Jullien; Jean-Charles de Castelbajac; the Athis Aviation museum; Christine Janodet, mayor of Orly; Marc Houalla, director, Paris-Orly airport; the Groupe ADP press and public relations team for Paris-Orly; the team at Groupe ADP's laboratory for the management of engineering and architecture; Haïm Korsia, chief rabbi of France and a Paris-Orly chaplain; Éditions de La Martinière.

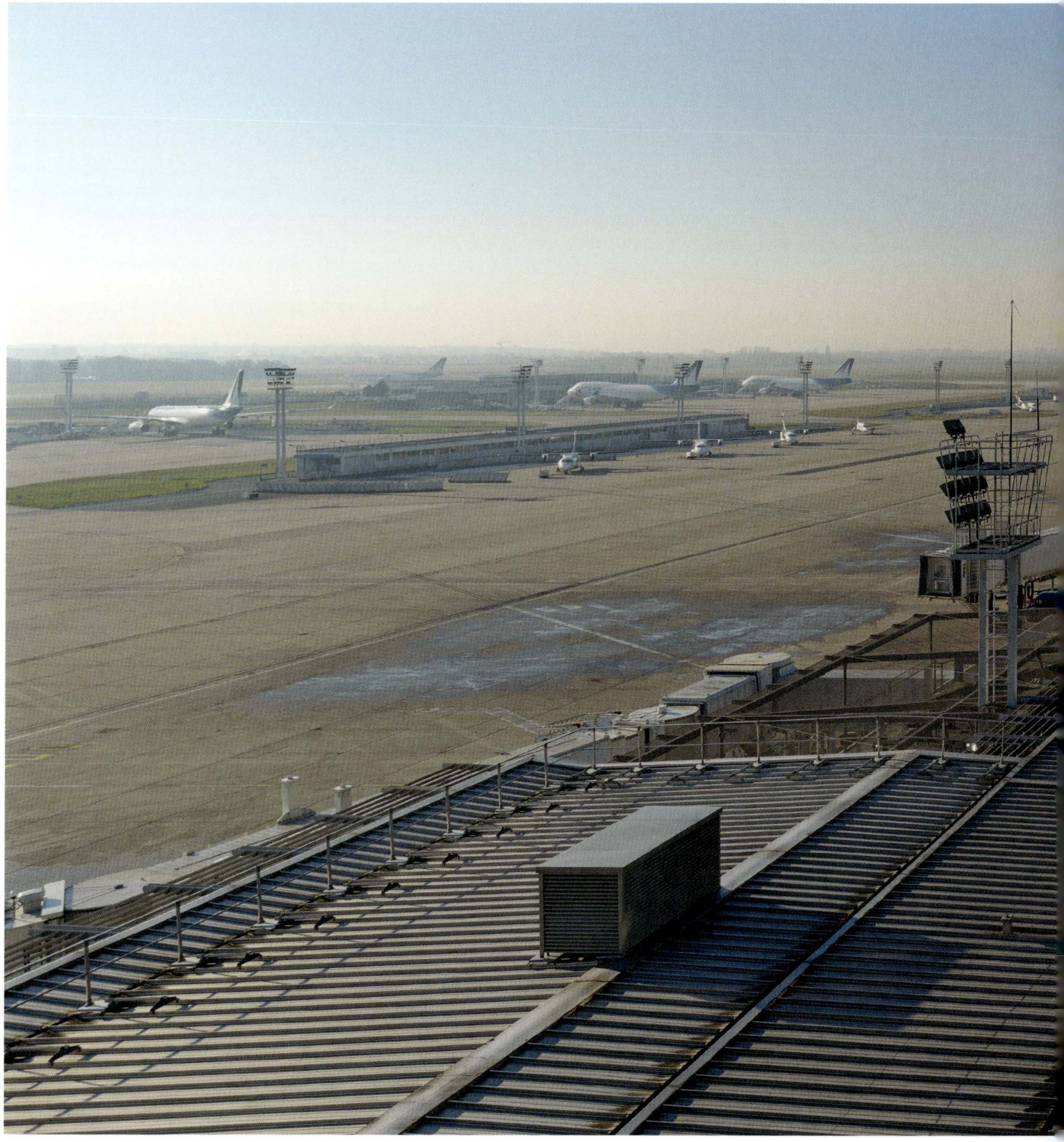

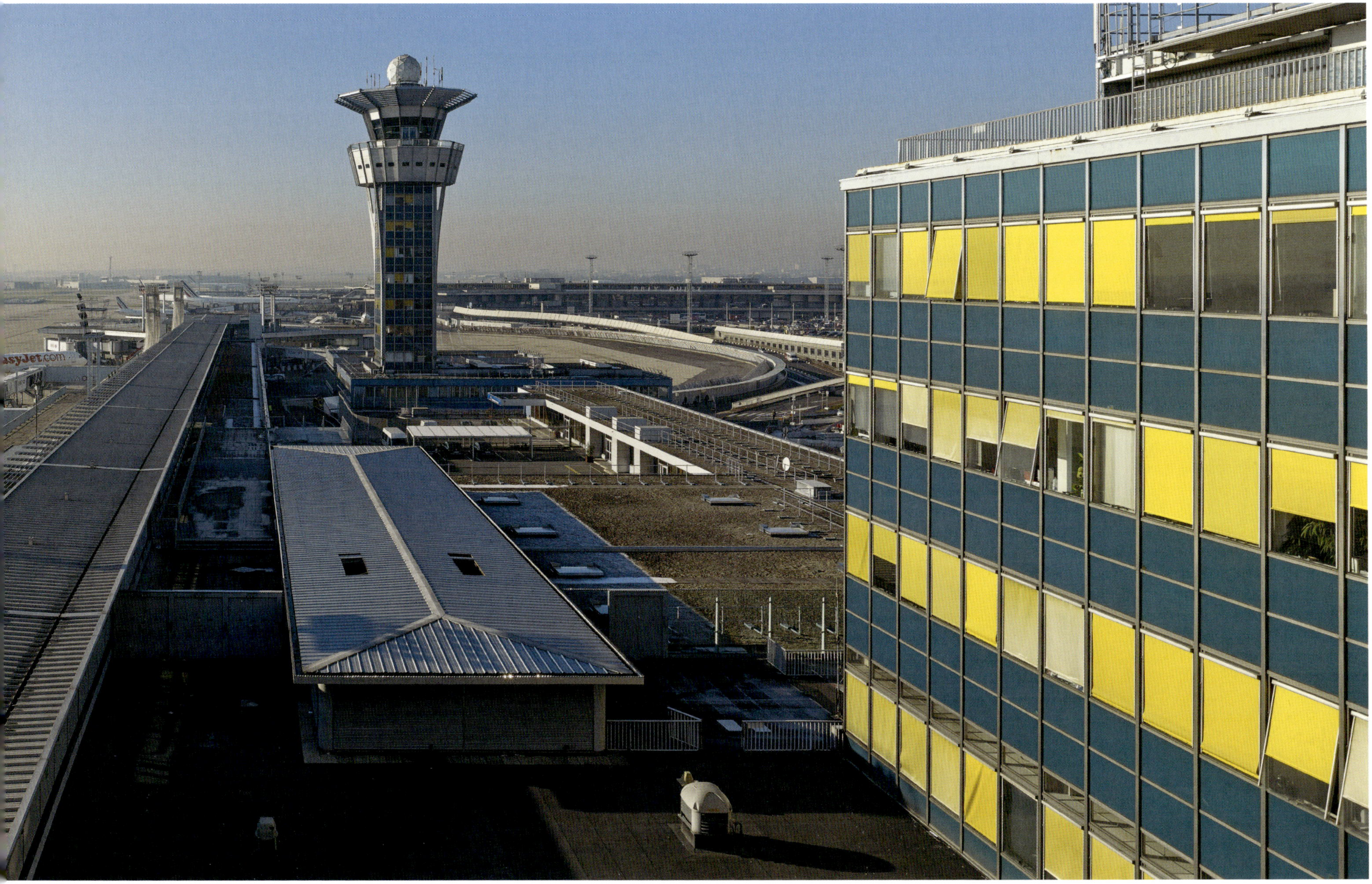

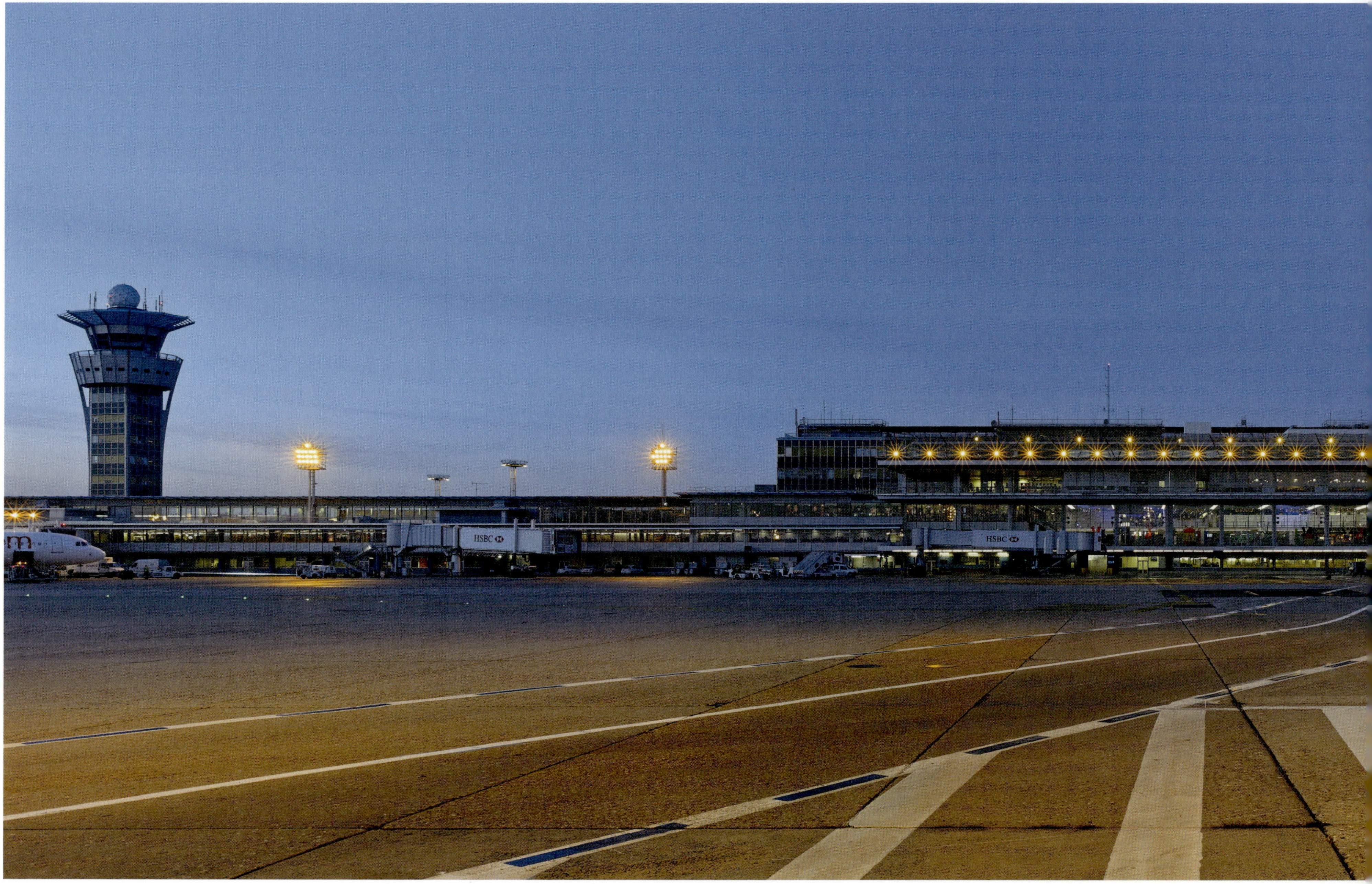
HSBC
HSBC

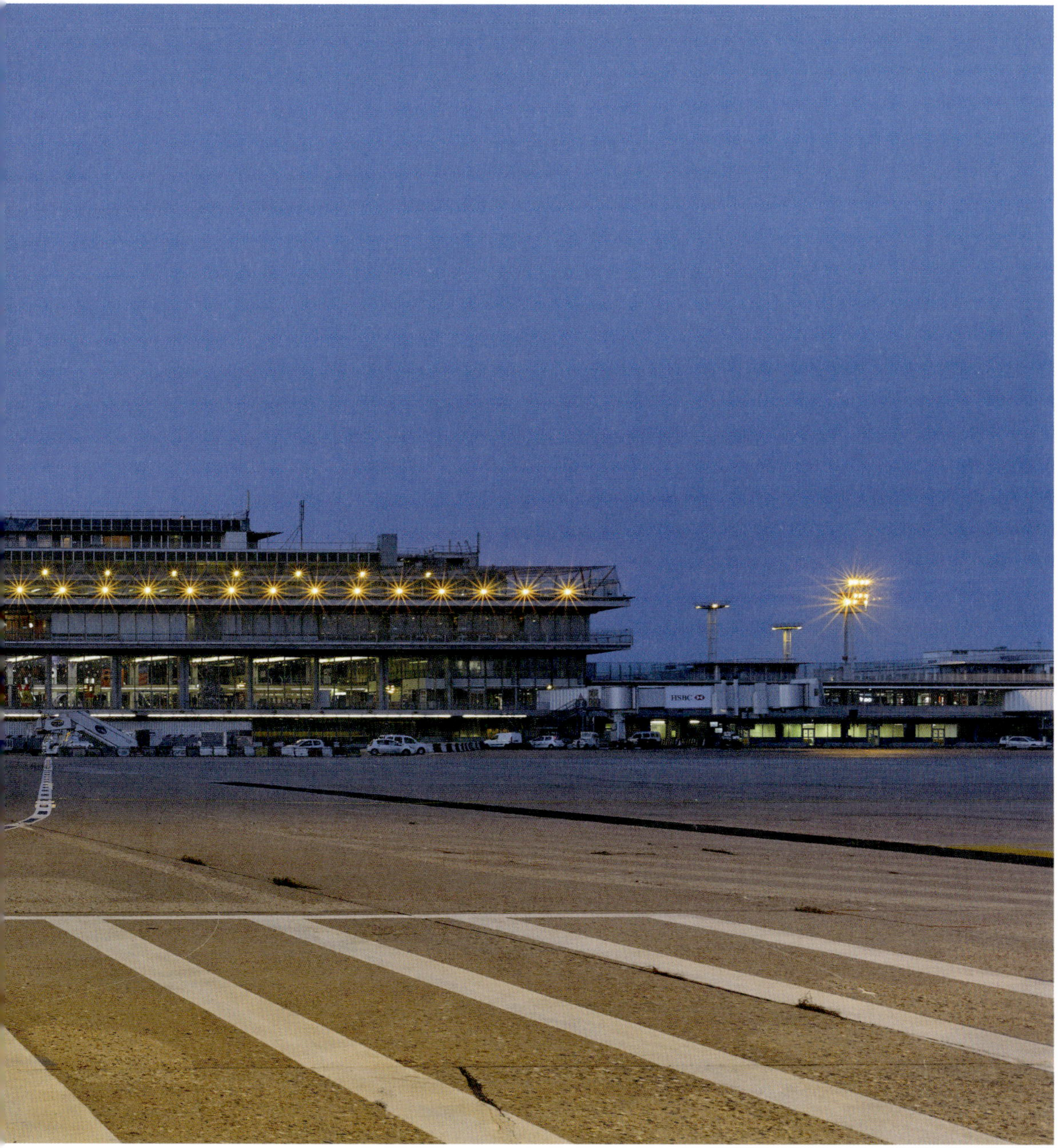

Photo credits

Cover and p.169: © Franck Bindefeld pour Aéroports de Paris SA

Aéroports de Paris SA: p.155, 173, 179; © Archives Aéroports de Paris: p.61 (bottom); © Artefacto: p.183 (top); © Vincent Bourilhon: p.116-117, 122, 123, 124, 125, 168, 174; © Pierre-Yves Brunaud: p.104, 113, 115, 128, 129, 130, 131, 133, 134, 135, 137, 138, 139, 140, 141, 144, 145, 147; © Sylvain Cambon for Aéroports de Paris SA: p.161; © Guilhem de Castelbajac: p.167 (right); © Bernard Charles/art-avia.eu: p.142, 143; © Collection Association anciens aérodromes*: p.20, 24, 25, 26, 27, 29 (upper left and above); © Collection V. Ferry: p.17, 21, 23; © Collection J.Y.Lorant: p.12, 31; D.R.: p.159 right; © Jean-Pierre Gaborit for Aéroports de Paris SA: p.120, 121, 160; © Groupe ADP/Photothèque: p.10, 28, 29 (right), 30, 32, 35, 36, 38, 39, 40, 41, 42, 43, 44, 45, 46, 47, 48, 49, 50, 51, 52, 53, 55, 56, 57, 58, 59, 60, 61 (upper right), 62, 63, 64, 65, 66, 67, 68 (left, upper and above), 69, 70, 71, 72, 73, 77, 78, 81, 82, 83, 84, 85, 86, 87, 88, 89, 90, 91, 92, 93, 94, 95, 96, 97, 98, 99, 100, 101, 102, 103, 108, 126, 127, 148, 149, 151, 152, 163, 165, 171, 175, 177, 178, 180, 181, 188-189, 190-191; © Clément Hurel © ADAGP Paris, 2017: p.68 (on the right); © Izusek: p. 159 (lower left); © Kara: p.183 (bottom); © Gwen Le Bras for Aéroports de Paris SA: p.4-5, 118, 119 (bottom), 159 (upper left), 167 (left); © Emile Luider/La Company for Aéroports de Paris SA: p.74, 156; © Bruno Pellarin for Aéroport de Paris SA: p.166; © Petit/Paris Match/Scoop: p.132; © Prod DB © Argos films/D.R.: p.68 (center); © Seignettelafontan.com for Aéroports de Paris SA: p.119 (above); © WikiCommons: p.15, 16, 18, 19, 22; © Valentin Yvon: p.6-7, 107, 109, 110, 111, 112, 162, 186.

*All images credited to the Collection Association Anciens Aérodromes are drawn from the resources of the association. (Siège social : Aérodrome de Merville-Calonne, Rue de l'Épinette, 62136 Lestrem, anciens-aerodromes.com)

Author: Frédéric Béniada
Translation from French: Florence and Mark Brutton
Image research: Emmanuelle Halkin
Graphic design and artwork: Élisabeth Welter

Sponsored by

GROUPE ADP

Copyright 2018, Éditions de La Martinière, an imprint of EDLM for the original and English translation.

Published in 2018 by Abrams, an imprint of ABRAMS. All rights reserved. No portion of this book may be reproduced, stored in a retrieval system, or transmitted in any form or by any means, mechanical, electronic, photocopying, recording, or otherwise, without written permission from the publisher.

FSC MIX Paper from responsible sources FSC® C057358

Printed and bound in Slovenia
10 9 8 7 6 5 4 3 2 1

Abrams books are available at special discounts when purchased in quantity for premiums and promotions as well as fundraising or educational use. Special editions can also be created to specification.

ABRAMS The Art of Books
115 West 18th Street, New York, NY 10011
abramsbooks.com

ISBN 978-1-4197-3091-7
Photoengraving: Turquoise

Printed in December 2017 by Gorenjski tisk storitve d.o.o. (Slovenia)